RACISM
101

Also by Nikki Giovanni

Black Feeling, Black Talk/Black Judgement
Re: Creation
Gemini
Spin a Soft Black Song
My House
A Dialogue: James Baldwin and Nikki Giovanni
Ego Tripping and Other Poems for Young Readers
A Poetic Equation: Conversations Between Nikki Giovanni
  and Margaret Walker
The Women and the Men
Cotton Candy on a Rainy Day
Vacation Time
Those Who Ride the Night Winds
Sacred Cows . . . and Other Edibles
Knoxville, Tennessee
Grand/Mothers (edited by Nikki Giovanni)

RACISM
101

NIKKI GIOVANNI

FOREWORD BY VIRGINIA C. FOWLER

QUILL
WILLIAM MORROW
NEW YORK

Some of these essays were previously published in magazines including: *Essence* ("Shooting for the Moon" and "Campus Racism 101"), *The Black Collegian* ("This Has Nothing to Do with You" and "Sisters, Too"), *Catalyst Magazine* ("A Letter from Nikki"), *The Upstart Crow Magazine* ("Giovanni on Shakespeare," retitled "I Plant Geraniums") *Harrison Happenings* ("Paper Dolls, Iron Skillets, Libraries, and Museums"), *Appalachian Community Fund Fifth Anniversary Journal* ("Coffee Signs"), *Wyoming High School Journal Icarus* ("Memories Are Selective"), *The Miami Herald* ("Griots"), *The Ohioana Quarterly* ("My Road to Virginia"), and *Lines* ("Architecture").

"Black Is the Noun" was previously published in *Lure and Loathing: Essays on Race, Identity, and the Ambivalence of Assimilation*, edited by Gerald Early (New York: Allen Lane/The Penguin Group, 1993).

"Dig," music by Miles Davis. Copyright © 1964 Prestige Music. Used by permission of Fantasy, Inc.

It is the policy of William Morrow and Company, Inc., and its imprints and affiliates, recognizing the importance of preserving what has been written, to print the books we publish on acid-free paper, and we exert our best efforts to that end.

Library of Congress Cataloging-in-Publication Data

Giovanni, Nikki.
    Racism 101 / Nikki Giovanni.
       p.   cm.
    ISBN 0-688-14234-6
    1. Giovanni, Nikki—Biography.   2. Afro-American women poets—20th century—Biography.   3. Afro-Americans—Social conditions.
4. Afro-Americans—Civilization.   5. Racism—United States.
I. Title.
PS3557.I55Z47   1994
811'.54—dc20
[B]   93 -29602
                                                      CIP

Printed in the United States of America

First Quill Edition

1 2 3 4 5 6 7 8 9 10

BOOK DESIGN BY PATRICE FODERO

FOREWORD

"A real writer," James Baldwin says in "Alas, Poor Richard," "is always shifting and changing and searching," a fact that often creates an "intensity of . . . bewilderment" in the writer's audience. But despite this inconvenience to readers, reviewers, and critics, "a real writer" will indeed challenge attempts to pigeonhole her or his work because, Baldwin continues, that "work is fatally entangled with his [or, presumably, her] personal fortunes and misfortunes, his personality, and the social facts and attitudes of his time."

Baldwin's observations have particular relevance to this most recent collection of essays by Nikki Giovanni, "a real writer" by anyone's definition. The essays brought together here span the past five years of the poet's life; they project her view of the world that her new perspective as a faculty member in a large research university affords her. Readers familiar with Giovanni's earlier life and work—both poetry and prose—will not perhaps be surprised by many of her reactions to being a member of one of society's most conservative institutions, though they will perhaps find it remarkable that this most iconoclastic and individualistic writer made a decision to accept a position in *any* institution. That the perspective afforded by this decision should find its initial expression in prose rather than poetry is hardly surprising; what *will*, perhaps, startle the reader of this collection is the decidedly poetic sensibility Giovanni brings to the many unpoetic subjects she addresses here. Emily Dickinson's famous dictum that the poet should "tell all the Truth but tell it slant" is certainly true of many of these essays, which work indirectly and figuratively to delineate "the truth" about education, educational institutions, racism, writing, and a host of other subjects.

The prophetic and truth-telling qualities that we associate with the poetry that came out of the Black Arts Movement of the sixties and early seventies are as much in evidence in these essays as they were in Giovanni's earliest and most "militant" poetry. But the changes wrought in American culture by the last twenty-five years are quite evident in the modulations of the voice that speaks from these pages. What is constant in Nikki Giovanni, from her first book of poems to this most recent collection, are the fundamental values that shape her vision of society, culture, and life itself: a belief in the necessity to fight injustice wherever it appears and in whatever form; a commitment to an historical perspective, to looking at the present with a fully informed sense of the past; a respect, often even a reverence, for the past and present struggles of African-American people; a desire to find underlying connections between and among people and events; and, of course, an abiding belief in the integrity and the power of the individual. Whether she is speculating about space exploration, indicting higher education for the inequities it perpetuates and its frequent failure to accomplish its mission, or offering her own version of a film about Malcolm X, these values inform her attempt to get at the fundamental core of the subject, the heart of the matter.

In form, most of these essays are like jazz compositions, relying on highly individualized improvisation to develop their themes. To reduce those themes to their essence is to miss altogether the meaning and significance of the essays, for Giovanni's *improvisatory performance* of her themes is what ultimately matters. It is also what constitutes the *art* of these essays. They are not the sort of academic essays we would normally expect to read on the subjects addressed here. No, these pieces are artistic expressions of a particular way of looking at the world, featuring a performing voice capable of dizzying displays of virtuosity. Like a jazz musician, she is both composer and performer, and the prose style she has created is as distinctive as a Charlie Parker's or a Nina Simone's.

Louis Armstrong once said that if you have to ask what jazz is, you'll never know. The same admonishment must be made to readers of this volume. Those who do know, however, should sit back and listen to the music.

Virginia C. Fowler

ACKNOWLEDGMENTS

I really suppose when you write a book like this everyone already understands that the ideas contained therein cannot help but belong to the author. Who the devil would write some of the things that I do other than me? Speaking of the devil, a well-known colloquial expression, I'd like to thank my son, Thomas, for talking over his concerns and my ideas with me. He is a good and patient listener and a forceful presenter of his own ideas. I must say I would not want to have had a son who would just roll over because someone older and with more degrees or something challenged him. Of course, he will never do well in life because he believes in truth, integrity, loyalty, and honor. Please buy this book so that he does not have to work for people who don't understand that.

I would also like to give my warmest thanks to the librarians at the Johnson Publications Company. They have been consistent and cheerful helpmates to me over the past couple of years, researching facts, ferreting out old articles, and offering leads for the few facts that I actually used in this book.

Obviously, without some editorial direction I would not have been able to at least make sense enough so that the academy, among others, could disagree. For that consistency of logic that was achieved, I thank Ginney Fowler. Probably, outside of those who birthed me, lived with me since birth, or whom I birthed, she best understands what I have tried to achieve with my writing. I would be remiss if I did not thank her for both the foreword and for a careful reading of this manuscript.

I thank my sister for the world's most wonderful Lemon Tart, which kept me going when I was stymied, and my Mother, who made grits and oysters when I was needing my mother.

Nikki Giovanni

CONTENTS

AUTHOR'S NOTE:

"IT'S ELEMENTARY, MY DEAR WATSON"

During that very hot summer of '93, I grilled a four-bone standing rib roast. I had purchased it in late spring, anticipating a visit from relatives, and when they had to change their plans, the roast went to the back of the freezer. I don't know about anyone else, but I clean house and garage and shed and freezer during seasonal change. The roast came to the front, but there didn't seem to be any special reason to turn on the oven ... and after all, a standing rib roast is special, so it kept not getting eaten. Finally, one day when a storm was brewing and it was too hot for the oven, I nonetheless decided to cook the roast. It was illogical, I know. I could have waited; I was no more special when I cooked it than when I was refusing to, but I soaked it in olive oil and soy sauce, sprinkled lots of garlic salt all around it, and packed the top with cracked pepper. I let the roast relax for almost three hours while I prepared the fire. I have a very basic Weber, so I was, by then, mentally prepared to throw away that piece of meat if my equipment couldn't do the job.

When my fire died to embers, I gently laid the roast on one side. The flames flared for about two minutes, then I turned it over. Two more minutes and I turned again. Same for the last side. Then I halved a lemon and squeezed the juice over the blackened parts. Spraying the flames down, I put the top on the Weber and went inside the house to finish the last pages of the biography of Adam Clayton Powell that I was reading.

I mention this because some of you may want to know how I put together this collection; or why it's called *Racism 101*, when many of these essays ostensibly have nothing to do with race; or why I repeat myself and my themes sometimes. I think I owe you an explanation: Any woman who would grill a standing rib roast would write this collection.

Writing is a conversation with reading; a dialogue with thinking. All conversations with older people contain repetition. Some of the ideas mean a lot to me and others are, to me, just interesting, so I both embrace and attack the ideas because I found them . . . well . . . delightful. I hope you do, too. I tried to vary by subject so you wouldn't be reading the same idea either in embrace or under attack, you know? I just wanted to write an interesting book and look at the world I inhabit. I'm a poet; I believe that the image will reveal itself. If the *Racism* is confusing, the *101* cannot be. Sherlock Holmes says, "Elementary." I think, "Basic." And the recipe is free.

I

PREFATORY:

"TO CATCH THE CONSCIENCE OF THE KING"

—WILLIAM SHAKESPEARE

GRIOTS

I must have heard my first stories in my mother's womb.

Mother loved a good story and my father told good jokes, but it was her father, Grandpapa, who told the heroic tales of long ago. Grandpapa was a Fisk University graduate (1905) who had majored in Latin. As he sometimes told the story, he had intended to be a diplomat until he met Grandmother, but that is probably another story altogether, he being Black and all in 1905 or thereabouts.

Grandpapa loved the stars. He knew the constellations and the gods who formed them, for whom they were named.

Grandpapa was twenty years the senior of Grandmother, so he was an old man when we were born. Grandmother's passion was flowers; his, constellations. One needn't have a great imagination to envision this courtship: the one with her feet firmly planted on earth, the other with his heart in the sky. It is only natural that I would love history and the gossip of which it is composed.

Fiction cannot take the place of stories. Aha, you caught me! Fiction is stories, you say. But no. Stories, at their best, pass along a history. It may be that there was no Ulysses with a faithful Penelope knitting and unraveling, but something representative of the people is conveyed. Something about courage, fortitude, loss, and recovery.

I, like most young ladies of color, used to get my hair done every Saturday. The beauty parlor is a marvelous thing. Every Saturday you got the saga of who was sleeping with whose husband; who was pregnant; who was abused by whose boyfriend or husband. Sometimes they would remember the children were there, but mostly the desire of the women to talk without the presence of the men overcame their desire to shield us from the real world.

My mother's family is from Albany, Georgia, but Grandmother and Grandpapa had moved to Knoxville, Tennessee. We four grandchildren spent our summers with Grandmother.

At night, when we were put to bed, my sister Gary and I would talk and sing and sometimes read under the covers using our Lone Ranger flashlight rings. Of course, we were caught. Grandmother would threaten us and take our rings. We would sneak out of our room, wiggling on our stomachs, to reach the window under which we sat and listened to Grandpapa and Grandmother talk.

Sitting under that window I learned that Eisenhower was not a good president; I learned that poll taxes are unfair. I heard Grandmother berate Grandpapa for voting Republican when "Lincoln didn't do all that much for colored people." I heard assessments of Black and white people of Knoxville and the world. No one is enhanced by this. I'm not trying to pretend they were; there were no stories of "the African" in my family, although I am glad there were in Alex Haley's.

We were just ordinary people trying to make sense of our lives, and for that I thank my grandparents. I'm lucky that I had the sense to listen and the heart to care; I'm glad they talked into the night, sitting in the glider on the front porch, Grandmother munching on fried fish and Grandpapa eating something sweet. I'm glad I understand that while language is a gift, listening is a responsibility. There must always be griots . . . else how will we know who we are?

II

"PLIGHTING TROTH BENEATH THE SKY"

—COUNTEE CULLEN

PAPER DOLLS, IRON SKILLETS, LIBRARIES, AND MUSEUMS

I used to cut out paper dolls, a thing I think no longer exists in the age of Barbie and Ken and those turtle things. My sister and I would sometimes draw our own clothes, color them, paste and glue wonderful accessories . . . but we never could get the tabs right . . . and the clothes fell off. Fortunately we were not easily discouraged, and Mommy always praised our efforts.

There are certain advantages to having an older sister. She took piano lessons first and played so well I knew it was pointless for me to try. Well, I tried but it was the kind of effort one gives when one knows one is doomed to second place. She also took French first so I learned the alphabet, numbers, and a few dirty words before I enrolled in school. Our father was a math whiz. Give him a few numbers and he'd see the sequence; give him a problem and he would solve it. Gary, my sister, inherited that trait from him. It's all I can do to keep my checkbook straight. All this is leading up to a point. I had to find things that I could do well. Kickball is not actually a sport by which one can earn a living; I was good at dodgeball, but my temper is not suited to being graciously hit. That left tennis and poetry.

Had I not lived in a world that had so little regard for the wishes of Black girls, I may have tried the tennis circuit. Althea Gibson had, after all, shown that it could be done, if one subscribes to role-model theories, but, irony of all ironies, my parents didn't like the travel. And anyway, I started to smoke in college, so that killed that. My task? To find something I loved that did not require me to change my physical habits while allowing me to grow emotionally and intellectually. No problem.

I've always loved libraries. Spending most summers in Knoxville, Tennessee, where I was born, I established a wonderful daily routine. Breakfast in the morning, tennis, shower, lunch, library. To be quite honest, I'm not now and never was a breakfast fan, but it would just break Grandmother's heart if you didn't eat, not something, but a bit of everything. I ultimately moved to Knoxville and attended Austin High. When I went to college I was, well, chubby. Three weeks after registration I had dropped twelve pounds and could actually see my cheekbones and distinguish my eyes. But then, being human, I missed Grandmother's breakfasts. Moral of this story: People complain about what they have until they don't have it; then they miss it.

I never envisioned being a librarian because of the math. Dewey and the others still confuse me. I, in fact, which I say without bragging, will dial 411 all day long because I refuse to keep a phone book that I cannot use anyway. I've always made friends with librarians so that they didn't mind getting the books I needed or wanted. I simply am a firm believer that if you have incompetence in an area, you should turn to people who have expertise. Which brings me to museums.

As a Black woman I never visited a museum until I enrolled at Fisk in Nashville. Knoxville didn't have any that Black people seemed to visit; Cincinnati, our hometown, had them but we never seemed welcome. Both my sister and I are collectors. Though neither of us had articulated it until fairly recently, we now realize that we grew up in museums. Because the Black community had no public place to deposit our memories, the churches and Colored Schools, the Masonic and other lodges, but mostly the homes in which we and our playmates lived, were museums. The photographs of men and women in the armed services from the Civil War to the present; the framed letter saying great-great-grandfather was entitled to a pension for his service to the country; the books signed by Booker T. Washington, Langston Hughes, James Weldon Johnson, W.E.B. Du Bois; the piece of silver or crystal from "the plantation." The needlepoint chairs, pillows that were embroidered, handkerchiefs with delicate work, the quilts . . . oh, the beautiful quilts filled with gunnysacks, old army blankets, bags that once held one hundred pounds of flour or coffee beans, which weighted you down when you went to bed. The Black community is a living museum. This Christmas Gary fried chicken in Grandmother's iron skillets. Grandmother had inherited them from Grandpapa's family. Those things can't be purchased today. It takes a generation just to get them properly seasoned. And a lifetime of love to understand that they are.

I PLANT GERANIUMS

I plant geraniums each spring. It's not that I am a gera-
nium lover or even a plant lover; it's just that at spring
there should be an acknowledgment of something new,
some rebirth, some faith in constant change. I don't par-
ticularly like grubs or Japanese beetles; I actually hate fly-
ing things. My allergies allow me to plant my tomatoes but
not to harvest them. Something about the fuzz that were
I willing and able to pay six hundred dollars, my derma-
tologist could explain exactly why I break out when I
touch it. I actually don't care. I'm quite content, in fact, to
press family and friends into tomato-picking service: "It's
my allergies, you know."

I'm not a critic, though I have been known to write a
book review or two. When younger, I actually thought my
opinion counted. I have since learned. When younger, I
thought one of the particulars of being "Homo sapiens"
was to communicate. I have not learned not to, though I
am cautious when I try. Life is far too serious to take

seriously. All the important things happen without our knowledge, consent, or active, conscious participation. We are conceived. We live. We die. We have no opinion on these subjects. Most of us don't even get to name ourselves. We can lie about our ages, but on the Gregorian or Chinese or Islamic calendar we are a certain age. That old expression, I think they call it a social lie, that "you don't look it or would never have thought you are . . ." takes away one of the crowning achievements of humans . . . that you survived. Of course, some people commit suicide to control the time of their deaths, but the end result is the same. Granting all that, which is, after all, not so much to grant, I support the concept of human life.

Shakespeare is lucky. There is an old African saying: "You are not dead until you are forgotten." Many groups share that belief, including some American Indians. The Euro-American must believe it because he works so hard to keep his history alive. It's fine by me. I hope, like Shakespeare, to one day be a *Jeopardy!* subject. I hope high school seniors quake at the fact that they have to take Giovanni before they graduate. I certainly can see the controversy over who actually wrote my poems; why did I never receive a "major" poetry award? These things get many a professor tenured, keeping many a family fed. One might even win promotion to "full" professor with the lucky and unusual discovery of some obscure grocery list proving once and for all, until deconstruction, that I do have false teeth. These things matter.

But I don't think Shakespeare had to worry about it. I think he had to write plays telling the king, "You are a fool" while keeping his head upon his shoulders. He had to tell the people who scrimped and saved to see his productions, "You are jealous, small-minded idiots who will

28

kill the one you love." He had to show his public that the savage was more noble than their pretentious societies while making them come back. He had to expose literal-mindedness for the foolishness that it is. Shakespeare was a working artist.

How could he have known that five or six hundred years later he would be required reading? Should he have foreseen this possibility and tempered his judgments to match? Should not he have considered the possibility that his words would be difficult to read, and should he there-fore have anticipated modern usage? Shouldn't we hold him to the same standards as the Constitution and Bible and bring him "up to date"? I think not. I think we should leave him in the brilliance of his expression. We need, we modern artists and critics, to do exactly what Shakespeare did. Write for now. Think for now. Express ourselves in our best possible vernacular for now. Will we be remem-bered? I doubt it. Most people are not remembered. And most people who would remember the people are not remembered. We have no true concept of what "Homo sapien" has forgotten, though surely some of it was good and some of it was useless.

Shelley or Keats, I always mess up which one, talked about tending his own garden. Or was it Voltaire? I plant geraniums. No one will remember that. I have an allergy to tomato fuzz. No one will care. I write poetry and some-times prose. No one will know me . . . let alone what I thought I did. But while I live, during this all too brief period between birth and death, my life and work have been meaningful to me. "The rest is silence."

REMEMBERING FISK ...
THINKING ABOUT DU BOIS

There were three things the children in my family, both immediate and extended, were expected to do: go to church each Sunday; clean our rooms each Saturday; and go to college. I never really gave a lot of thought to which college. I think I more or less had decided the lot of the toss would make my decision. My parents were graduates of Knoxville College; my grandfather was a graduate of Fisk University; my sister was attending Central State in Ohio. To some degree, like all younger people, I did not want to attend any school where there had been a previous person. I had spent entirely too much of my life hearing about being so-and-so's sister, so-and-so's daughter, so-and-so's grandbaby. I was rather looking forward to going to places unknown, forging my own path, cutting new ground and all that. I attended Fisk.

The Ford Foundation played a small but significant part in my decision. It seems, if memory serves me well, that they had sponsored a study about taking talented students from high school early, as early as the sophomore year, testing them for intellectual readiness, and encouraging certain institutions to accept them as college freshmen. I was a junior when either Miss Delaney, my English teacher, or Mrs. Stokes, my French teacher, mentioned the program to me. Most of us, it is fair to say, are bored in high school. I jumped at the chance.

I had gone, by train, with my grandfather to Philadelphia to visit my aunt and uncle. I remember Philadelphia being murderously cold. I was living with my grandparents in Knoxville, Tennessee, and, to keep the record straight, we had gotten Austin High's permission for me to miss classes for a week or two. Both Grandpapa and I had forgotten that the test was coming up. I hadn't been in Philly for more than three or four days when Grandmother called and said I had to come home. Frankly, I was a bit unhappy, but I have always liked travel and I have always liked traveling alone, so the thought of leaving Philly was balanced by a twelve-hour ride on the train. I went back to Knoxville.

The test seemed like a normal test to me. Miss Brooks, our school librarian, administered it. I remember she teased me about not having enough squares to fill in my name, "Yolande Cornelia Giovanni"; I left off the "Jr." The only question I remember was a true/false: Fifty thousand Frenchmen can't be wrong. I said false. The correct answer is true. I still think the majority should not rule, but that's a different discussion.

We also had to fill out the name of the school where we would like our results sent. I had considered Swarthmore as a college I would like and I had considered Mount Holyoke, but they were not among those listed. I recognized Fisk and, with one of these real devil-may-care motions, checked it. I didn't think I'd done that well, anyway. A few weeks later I received a letter and an application. Still cool, I filled it out. Grandmother and Grandpapa were pleased; we called Mommy to tell her. I know now her first reaction must surely have been, "How are we going to send two girls to school?" but she was cool and made very encouraging noises. My father was a bit disappointed, as he had planned to come to my graduation. Gus, my father, had not been to a high school graduation since his own. My sister Gary had finished early in the summer and was at Central State, and now it looked like I was going to Fisk. I did.

Fisk was beautiful then: the lawn around the library, the majesty of Jubilee Hall, the comfort and very waxy smell of the chapel. There was no way to not love it, which I did. There was no way not to rebel, which I did. There was a men's dormitory, Du Bois Hall, which had, in fact, a painting of Frederick Douglass hanging. Odd. But not really challengeable. I, as did all young Black people of my age, knew who Du Bois was. Knew that he was alive and living in Ghana. Knew that he had walked these halls; sat in some of these classrooms; studied in the very same library. You could even still meet people who had known him, could tell stories about him. It was thrilling. I have always been a book freak. To this very day I am seeking an autographed copy of *The Souls of Black Folk*. I wanted to go to the library and touch and read from the first editions, but being a lowly freshman with no stack privileges, that was not to be. Fortunately for me, paperbacks were available and I reread, in one case, and read, in the others, all that he had written.

There is a lot to learn from writers, if I may use a cliché. We learn the information they have to share; we also learn their style and methods of writing, but for someone like me we learn that they are . . . that they did what they thought they should do . . . that they followed the dictates of their own hearts and minds.

Du Bois was a fearless man. He was not intimidated by white or Black; he did not gladly suffer any fool. He worked at colleges and with institutions based on his respect for them, not on whether he needed a job. If there was any one thing I learned from him it was, in fact, a relearning . . . you must do, say, and write that which you believe to be true. What others think can be of no significance.

Du Bois has stood the test of time. Though his late-life disappointments overwhelmed his logic, though he let his love of America and its failure to return that love turn him bitter, he was an intellectual of action, a rare combination. He showed us all that matters is that we contribute what we can where we can.

When I returned to Fisk, long after my graduation, long after presidents, deans of students, boards of directors had come and gone, there was a statue of Du Bois standing at Fisk. I am proud of my alma mater; we finally had the courage to salute one of our great sons who was and will remain "ever on the altar."

THE SIXTIES

A REVIEW OF *MY SOUL IS RESTED: MOVEMENT DAYS IN THE DEEP SOUTH REMEMBERED* BY HOWELL RAINES

My personal problem with what is called "the sixties," roughly that period between the Brown decision of the Supreme Court (1954) and the election of Richard Nixon (1968), is that I think we won.

I was born in a small town nestled in the mountains of eastern Tennessee, Knoxville, and grew up in a midwestern city that prided itself on being the "Gateway to the South." I have vivid memories of WHITE LADIES and COLORED WOMEN signs from Knoxville; Cincinnati didn't have signs—it didn't have to—you were simply ignored. My mother tells the story of going Christmas shopping with my godmother, my sister, and me when I was a little girl. She and my godmother, Edna Westfield, decided to take us to lunch at Dows Drugstore. We sat at the counter— two women and two little girls—and we sat and sat. Mommy says I said, "I'm thirsty," and the girl behind the counter finally slid a glass of water to us. Slid—not served—not given. We understood the error and left. I don't consciously remember the incident, but then I am not knowledgeable about the memory of the gene. There is a drugstore in a suburban Cincinnati area called Glendale. In the village square you park your car and walk to the drugstore, window-shopping, maybe stopping by the train station—all those things a family does on a Sunday in the fifties. We wanted, as kids do, ice cream, so we went to the drugstore. My father, who was a very friendly sort of fellow with a great grin, asked if we could eat the ice cream there. The clerk said, probably quite nicely, "*No.*" "Well then," said Gus, "we'll order five double cones" and proceeded to pick flavors. The clerk, most likely happy that an ugly event had been avoided, made up the order. When he finished, my father looked at him and said, "Now, eat them." It was a small rebellion as rebellions go—but it was a rebellion. I don't mention my parents because they led the march for equal rights. I mention them because the utter pain at being subjected to that level of unreasonable and incomprehensible humiliation was multiplied by parents all over this country and is still being faced by Black parents in South Africa. There is something radically wrong about being unable to shop and grab a snack, or take a Sunday drive and stop for ice cream—there is something insidious in your child's wanting to see *Snow White and the Seven Dwarfs* and your having to explain it's showing at the white theater—or in a parent's guiding a child to the colored drinking fountain or the colored toilet or the colored waiting room.

It's become quite fashionable to berate the sixties. "All you did was get a cup of coffee," they like to say. All the sixties did, in reality, was save the political entity we know as the United States from self-destruction. That Jimmy Carter, a poor white boy from rural Georgia, sat in the

White House is a testimony to the impact of the effort of Black people. And we seem to be the last to understand that. Linda Brown was a little Black girl whose parents sued the school board of Topeka, Kansas, for equal education. I have no idea, and won't until Linda writes her book, whether her mother or father was more instrumental in the suit. They sued and the Warren Court reached a unanimous decision that separate was inherently unequal. Rosa Parks was not just a little old lady with tired feet. She was a moving force in the Montgomery NAACP; she was an active club woman. She was also not the only person arrested for protesting bus discrimination. She was, however, the person known in the community for her work as well as for her temperament—she was known to be both dedicated and committed. She was a reasonable woman. If *Mrs. Parks* was arrested, the Black community, from the doctor to the desperate, from the most honored to the least secure, from the professional to the pimp, understood not that something was deeply wrong—the Black community from 1619 to 1993 understands something as being wrong—but that some resolution must be sought. Martin Luther King, Jr., being the youngest, most articulate, and to a large degree most neutral figure in Montgomery, began to speak for the rightful aspirations of not only Montgomery but Black America. Montgomery was not the first boycott, nor the first mass protest. It simply produced the leader who was able to place that small community in Alabama in a world perspective. The rightful aspirations of Montgomery were felt not only in the United States but all over planet earth where Black people were being held down by whites and ultimately where the powerful and rich are holding down the powerless and poor. *My Soul Is Rested: Movement Days in the Deep South*

Remembered is in the best tradition of the sixties. For those of us who are Black writers, it's almost ironic that the spoken word, in journalism, sociology, historical remembrances, is playing such a prominent role. Oral tradition, when Black Americans, Africans, Indians, and Hispanics practice it, is used as evidence of our "lower cultural development." When oral tradition is practiced by white journalists and sociologists, it is considered a new and exciting form. I am glad, however, that whites have once again discovered we are right. We are right in our moral outrage and we are right in our expression of it.

Howell Raines, a journalist, took his tape recorder south to record recollections of the movement days. People who would never write a book but who are great practitioners of the oral tradition tell their story.

Martin Luther King, Jr., is a personification of the sixties. His face, open and unafraid—his words, clear, compassionate, yet uncompromising, led a people—the Americans—into an examination of its soul. Risking his life, and ultimately losing it, King proved that words speak as loudly as action; that this nation and perhaps this world, because of the cancer of racism, was incapable of reaching the Christian idea of love. And by showing the barbarity of that incapability, he moved us all to a clearer understanding that we ultimately all share the same desire to live. King at first was not the American ideal of a hero. He was short; heroes were tall. He was Black; heroes were white. He was articulate; heroes mumbled. He led those without hope; heroes moved alone. Heroes after World War II were existential; King was committed to clear ideas of right and wrong. He led the Montgomery Improvement Association to victory and formed the Southern Christian Leadership Conference. What was wrong in Alabama was wrong in Georgia and Florida, in Chicago and New York City. "If violence was wrong in America," challenged Malcolm X, "then it was wrong abroad." "Why are we sent," asked Stokely Carmichael, "to defend our Motherland but taught not to defend our Mothers?" King was the most important public man to disavow the war in Vietnam. He was the first public man to speak of the equality of women and youth. He was a Daniel in a den not of lions—for lions are honorable beasts—but wolves. The packs howled for his flesh. They bit at his spirit. There is an old gospel song that says, "I've been lied on, cheated, talked about, mistreated, 'buked, scorned, talked about sure as I'm born; up, down, almost leveled to the ground, [but] long's I got King Jesus I don't need anybody else." King embodied the gospel songs and lived the Christian life. He was, while from man, clearly not of him. He shaped this age as neither Eisenhower nor Kennedy; John Foster Dulles nor Robert McNamara; Richard Nixon nor Joseph McCarthy could ever hope to. He was not a leader like Hitler, who hated; nor a wheeler-dealer like Franklin Roosevelt, who could care; but he was the man who gave reason once again to why the earth spins on its axis or why the sunbeams play on the noses of little barefoot children. He gave to us all the life-affirming concept of redemptive love. It is so regrettable that Howell Raines, because King was dead, was unable to include his words. Yet all the words in *My Soul Is Rested* are in fact King's—from the title to the last embrace Ralph Abernathy gives King.

I first heard Martin Luther King when he gave the commencement address at Knoxville College shortly after the Montgomery boycott. He loved to tell the story of the old woman he saw walking down the street one day. "Sister, you are old," he said. "You don't have to walk. Everyone will understand if you take the bus." The old lady shook her head no: "Son, I ain't walking for myself," she replied. "I'm walking for my grandchildren. My feets is tired; but my soul is rested." She continued her journey home.

Like a newly paved road with no speed limits and no restraints, *My Soul Is Rested* encourages the reader to speed on. It's a smooth easy read into an area that is still not fully explored. There are many more people to talk with, there are many more stories to be shared. The old folks used to say, "The half ain't never been told." But we are beginning. The real heroes of all periods are largely unsung and untold. Howell Raines has talked with people who shaped a great period. No matter that the ignorant, the indifferent, and the insensitive deride the contributions of Black men and women—we have known heroes—and heroic moments. It is for us, the cultural conveyors, to continue to explore what was the problem and what is the solution. Nothing in the sixties takes away the problems of the seventies, eighties, or nineties, or alleviates the pain of the post–World War II era. The sixties, however, solved the problems of the sixties—overt and lawful segregation; lynching; bombing; the wanton and capricious murder of Blacks by whites. As long as there are human beings, there will be problems in relationships. As long as there are men and women who shared their lives with the movement and their hopes with the Howell Raineses, there will be solutions.

Life is not a problem similar to science or mathematics where solutions can be discerned and tested. Life is a process where people mix and match, fall apart and come back together.

Today's clouds can never deny yesterday's beautiful

sunset. The inconvenience of today's storms can never turn us from tomorrow's harvest. We plant, we reap, we *try* because we are human. We hope, we continue. Our soul is rested, but it will have to get up in the morning and start again.

BLACK IS THE NOUN

It is late. The poet has just opened her second pack of cig-
arettes. The poet smokes like a chimney. She fears the day
when the possession of cigarettes, not just their use, will be
illegal. The light is on in her den, though her window blinds
are closed. She did not wear her seat belt today. They know.
She knows they know. Contemplating her fingernails, she
notices, to her horror, a speck of grease. She has, once again,
eaten fried chicken. It won't be long before they come for
her. What should she do? Finding no answer, she ambles to
the refrigerator, opens the freezer, and takes out peach sor-
bet. If she must go, she will go her way.

"I'VE HAD MY FUN . . . IF I DON'T GET WELL ANY MORE."
—J. MCSHANE

I knew I was old when, one evening last spring, I was
driving from Blacksburg to Princeton to attend a party. I
had finished early but a friend was driving with me and she
couldn't get off from work. We left about five-thirty in the
evening, driving my car, a candy-apple-red MR2. We had
on our normal driving garb, jeans and T-shirts. I am al-
ways cold, so I had on a sweatshirt. We were short-
coiffeured, medium-nailed, no-makeup, modern sort of
women on a fun drive to a fun place. We stopped for
coffee, smoked, munched the sandwiches we had made—
were, in other words, going about our business.

Ginney has two talents that I not only do not possess

but do not aspire to: She can spell and she can read a map. My idea of getting around is to go to the farthest point and make the appropriate ninety-degree turn. For example, in order to reach Princeton from Blacksburg, I would go to Washington, D.C., and turn left. But Ginney can read a map, so she angled us onto the Pennsylvania Turnpike, around Philadelphia, and into the New Jersey Turnpike. I don't like to be picky about things because I lack certain skills myself, but I do think it is not asking too much for employees to know where things are located. You know, you go into Krogers looking for, say, tomato puree. You would expect to find this in the canned vegetable section, only it isn't. It's located with sauces. You ask someone wearing a Krogers shirt and you should get that answer. You expect the turnpike officials who take your money at the toll booths to know which exit to take for something as well known as Princeton.

I have an aunt, well actually I have two aunts, but I only want to talk about one of them. My aunt, and I will not designate which, has trouble with her night vision. She is not quite as blind as a bat but she . . . well . . . has trouble. And there are, possibly, these genetic transfers. I don't think I've reached that stage yet, but sometimes it's difficult to see what exactly the signs are saying. It had gotten quite dark, we had stopped for coffee several times, and I, as driver, was happy to be on a turnpike with large green signs. When we were handed off from the Pennsylvania to the New Jersey, I asked the woman in the booth which exit I should take for Princeton. Had she just said, "Honey, I ain't got no idea where no Princeton is. It's been a long day and nothing has gone right. My left foot is hurting 'cause I cut that corn, but it's not healing right and maybe I have diabetes. You know, when a corn won't heal, that's a sign of diabetes. My mother had sugar and she lost her whole leg right up to the knee . . ." or something like that, I would have been understanding. "Yes," I would have said, "I've heard that corns that won't heal are a sign of sugar. My mother's best friend, Ann Taylor, from over in Knoxville, was just telling me about it when I was passing through last June." And she and I could have visited a bit while Ginney looked at the map and plotted our course. But no, she says, with authority, "Take exit nineteen," and we set out with the confidence of the innocently assured.

We were lost immediately; there was nothing that made sense on that exit, it was three-thirty in the morning, and, worst of all, I began to despair. We turned the light on in the car so that Ginney could see the map, but, golly, those lines are very, very small and the car was in motion, and bingo! The blue lights were shining in the back of me. I pulled over, popped the Dells tape out of the cassette, ground out my cigarette, grabbed my seat belt, and waited for the highway patrolman. "Your registration and license, please." I had the registration with my gas card in the front, but my driver's license was in my purse in the trunk. I looked up to explain my problem when he turned his flashlight into the car. He saw two McDonald's coffees, an ashtray full of cigarettes, and us . . . two lost, tired, old ladies. "Where are you coming from?" he asked. "Roanoke, Virginia." I always answer Roanoke because nobody knows where Blacksburg is. "How long have you been on the road?" "Since about five-thirty. We're lost. We're trying to get to Princeton." "Well," he explained. "you're way out of your way. You've got another fifty miles to go." He gave us directions and said, "Drive carefully." "I'll get my driver's license now," I offered. "Oh no, ma'am. You all just get where you're going. Have a safe evening."

Something in me clicked. A few years ago he would have given me a ticket. A few years ago whether I was lost or not I would have been written up. But we were just two little ol' ladies in what he probably thought was my son's car in the middle of the night trying to get to Princeton. I turned to Ginney: We are old. He saw old women. You drive.

"GOING TO CHICAGO . . . SORRY BUT I CAN'T TAKE YOU."
—W. BASIE

In *Star Trek II: The Wrath of Khan*, Khan, a criminal Kirk was responsible for putting on some planet way the hell out of nowhere, finally makes his escape. He is living for only one reason: He wants to kill Kirk. Khan and Kirk fool around for a couple of hours while Khan tortures and kills people and . . . finally . . . gets the *Enterprise* in his grip. Spock, of course, sees the problem and goes to the rescue. The awful weapon is turned on Khan and he is killed. But wait! Khan will have the last word even after death. Khan has trapped the *Enterprise* and it will implode because the crystals it needs cannot feed the engine. They all will die, and Khan, the evil Ricardo Montalban, whom I actually liked in *Fantasy Island,* will prove that evil triumphs over good even when evil can't be there to gloat about it.

Spock knows the answer, but Kirk cannot bear to see his friend give his life. Spock understands that either he gives his life or they'll all give their lives. He sneaks away from Kirk only to encounter McCoy. He uses the Spock maneuver to knock McCoy out, but at the last minute whispers: "Remember." And does his mind meld. Spock steps into the chamber, feeds the engine, and awaits his death. By now Kirk is on the deck, upset, quite naturally, about losing Spock. "The needs of the many," Spock says, "outweigh the needs of the few . . . or in this case, the one. I will always be your friend." He gives Kirk the Spock sign with the split fingers and dies. The next thing we see is Spock's funeral service and the *Enterprise* pushing his casket out into space. By this time I am embarrassing my son by actually heaving in the theater. I cannot believe Spock is dead. I will not accept it. But Tom points out to me that Spock's casket is headed for the Genesis planet. *Star Trek III: The Search for Spock* will bring him back. I cannot see it. If he's dead, how can he come back to life? In all our myths only one man was able to do that. But Spock did tell McCoy something: "Remember."

I love *Star Trek*s. They are nothing less than Greek myths of heroic people doing extraordinary deeds with style and wit. No one on the good ship *Enterprise* will ever be short of courage. The television series, which was actually quite short-lived, marked a new era in television by obliging audiences to respect—and even to admire—differences among people. They talked to rocks in "The Huerta" and spirits in "The Companion"; they came back to defy death at the O.K. Corral by not recognizing the power of bullets; they stopped a war between two planets by making them confront the reality and pay the price of the killing; they gave us television's first interracial kiss. But Spock said: "Remember."

The Search for Spock opens with Kirk and McCoy meeting Spock's father with a flag. Spock's Mom is Jane Wyatt, formerly married to Jim Anderson on *Father Knows Best*. No one ever mentions the divorce, but when you see how the kids came out you could easily see why she might have wanted to make her way to another planet. Mrs. Spock, Jane, is not seen. Since she is human, she's probably off crying her eyes out over losing her only child. Ambassador Spock, the Vulcan, is not emotional, so he stands to talk. "Where are his memories?" Ambassador Spock asks. He knows his son is dead, and he can accept that. But where are his memories? Kirk and McCoy have no idea what he is talking about. "My son was a great man," Ambassador Spoke all but bellows. "His memories are valuable to us. We can store them so that others will learn from what he knew. You must find his body and retract from his brain his memories."

Star Trek perfectly epitomizes the sixties. You had a courageous white boy; a logical Vulcan; an Asian scientific transportation officer; an Irish, emotional doctor; and, the ultimate genius of *Star Trek,* Uhura, a Black woman who was the voice of the entire Federation. Toni Morrison once wrote: "The Black woman is both a ship and a safe harbor." Uhura proved that. Of all the possible voices to send into space, the voice of the Black woman was chosen. Why? Because no matter what the words, the voice gives comfort and welcome. The Black woman's voice sings the best notes of which earthlings are capable. Hers is the one voice that suggests the possibility of harmony on planet earth. Scholars are now studying what made the slavers bring females on the slave ships. The slavers could not have been so stupid as to think they could get as much work from a woman as from a man. There is the theory that since the women ran the markets and worked the farms, the white man understood that in order for his agriculture to prosper, he would need the women. I think not. I think there was a cosmic plan; a higher reason. In order to have a *civilization,* the Black woman was needed.

So that one day forgiveness would be possible, the Black woman was needed. I need not, I'm sure, point out the fact that the first Black child born in what would become the United States was a Black female. The first poet. But more, I believe the first voice to be lifted in song was the voice of a Black woman. It may have been the "faith of our fathers," but it was our mothers who taught it to us. And when that faith is transformed, what do we have? A half earthling/half other-world being, saying to the doctor: "Remember."

Like Alex Haley's ancestor, who preserved his past by passing along his name, the slaves told their story through song. Isn't that why we sing "Swing Low, Sweet Chariot"? Isn't that why we know "Pass Me Not, Oh Gentle Savior"? Isn't that the reason our legacy is "You Got to Walk This Lonesome Valley?" "Were You There When They Crucified My Lord?" To Du Bois, the spirituals were sorrow songs, perhaps because he saw himself as so different from the slaves who sang them. But the spirituals were not and are not today sorrow songs but records of our history. How else would a people tell their story if not through the means available? We made a song to be a quilt to wrap us "in the bosom of Abraham." "Over my head, I see trouble in the air. . . . There must . . . be a God, somewhere." We knew "he didn't take us this far to leave us." We brought a faith to the barbarians among whom we found ourselves and the very humbleness of our souls defeated the power of their whips, ropes, chains, and money. "Give yourself to Jesus." Not your money, not a new church that you will sit in with other white people like yourself, not a new organ, none of those things . . . yourself. And all we had was a song and a prayer. Who would have remembered us had we not raised our voices?

Had Spock been a Black American, his father would have gone to church to ask the Lord for help. And his help would have come like the strength that came to Emmett Till's mother: "I know that's my boy," when the sheriff asked what she could contribute to the trial of Till's killers. "I know it's my boy," Mrs. Bradley, Till's mother, said when she opened the casket. "I want the world to see what they did to my boy." Didn't she roll the rock away? Two thousand years ago the Angels said: *"He is not here."* Mrs. Bradley said: "Here is my boy. Look." And the world was ashamed. Spock told McCoy to remember. And McCoy didn't even know what he had.

They went in search of the body and, movies being movies, they found a young Vulcan boy on Genesis and brought him home. But McCoy had the memories all along. He just didn't know what he had.

"ALTHOUGH YOU HAPPY, YOU BETTER TRY TO GET ALONG. MONEY WON'T CHANGE YOU, BUT TIME IS TAKING YOU ON."

—J. BROWN

Much evidence to the contrary, I am a sixties person. It's true that I didn't do tie-dyed T-shirts or drugs, and I never went to jail. I argued a lot in coffeehouses and tried at one point to be a social drinker. It didn't work. I can't hold liquor at all. But I was nonetheless a sixties person and continue to be today because I actually believe in the people. That was never just rhetoric to me, though it has often been my undoing. Believing in the people is dangerous, because the people will break your heart. Just when you know in your heart that white people are not worth a tinker's damn and the future depends on us, some Black person will come along with some nihilistic crap that makes you rethink the whole thing.

I was never more than a foot soldier and not a very

good one at that. I observed and I wrote. And the more I observed, the more amazed I was by our need to deny our own history . . . our need to forget, not to remember. The contradictions were especially evident to me, perhaps, because I attended Du Bois's school, Fisk University. How ironic that Fisk's Jubilee Singers kept the spirituals alive, yet the students at Fisk were anxious to deny that their ancestors were slaves; if people were to be believed, nobody but me ever had slaves in their family.

The fact of slavery is no more our fault than the fact of rape. People are raped. It is not their choice. How the victim becomes responsible for the behavior of the victimizer is well beyond my understanding. How the poor are responsible for their condition is equally baffling. No one chooses to live in the streets; no one chooses to go to sleep at night hungry; no one chooses to be cold, to watch their children have unmet needs. No one chooses misery, and our efforts to make this a choice will be the damnation of our souls. Yet such thinking is one of the several troubling legacies we have inherited from Du Bois.

Du Bois needed to believe that he was different. That if only the "better" white people would distinguish between "better" Black folk, "the talented tenth," then together they could make a "better" person. I think not. The normal ninety have to be respected for the trials and tribulations they have endured. They've been " 'buked and they've been scorned." They bore the lash while they cleared the fields, planted, and created in this wilderness. Am I against books and learning? Hardly. But just because my tools are words, I do not have the right to make mine the only tools. It is disturbing that wordsmiths like Henry Louis Gates, Jr., can say to those of physical prowess, "the odds are against your [succeeding in professional athletics]" (in a recent article in *Sports Illustrated*). The odds are more against any young man or woman of color being tenured at Harvard. Gates was not deterred in his determination to succeed in his chosen field, and he does not have the right to discourage others. Those young men on city playgrounds know that, indeed, basketball is the way out. Without that skill no school would be interested in them . . . no high school . . . no college. The academically excellent can use their words to sneer, but the young men know that's the only open door. Is it right? I think not. I would like to see choice come into everybody's life. But there are not good choices on the streets these days. The conservatives don't care, and the Black intellectuals are trying to justify the gross neglect of the needs of Black America. The Thomas Sowells, the Shelby Steeles no more or less than the Clarence Thomases and the Louis Sullivans are trying mighty hard to say, "I am not like them." We know that, we who are "them." We also know that such conservatives have no character. We know they are in opportunistic service. The very least they owe is the honesty that says, "I got here distinguishing myself from you." Clarence is against affirmative action? Shelby is against affirmative action? Since when? Since the people fought so that neither of these men would have to die for their choice of wives? So that Yale would admit a poor boy from Pin Point, Georgia? When did affirmative action become an insult? Shortly after you were granted tenure at your university? You don't like being made to feel you can honestly do your job because affirmative action made someone hire you? There is a solution. Quit. You think life is hard for you because you're viewed as a group? Try living in Newark or D.C. or Harlem and knowing that you will never be allowed by what Margaret Walker calls "those unseen creatures who tower over us omnisciently and laugh" to realize your dreams and potential.

Am I blaming Du Bois for his children? You bet. The Black conservatives belong to Du Bois. Booker T. Washington, born in slavery, reared in the coal-mining districts of West Virginia, walked his way to Hampton, worked his way through the Institute, labored in the red clay of Alabama among some of the most vicious white folks outside of Mississippi to build Tuskegee; he tried to empower Black folks. Is there a quarrel with the Atlantic Exposition speech? Somebody, other than the Black conservatives, show me where this nation is not still "as separate as the fingers of a hand" and how we would not all be better off if we would "come together as a fist" for economic development. Du Bois wanted to vote? So do we all. Didn't Martin Luther King, Jr., have something to say about "Southern Negroes not being allowed to vote while Northern Negroes have nothing to vote for?" Didn't Frederick Douglass ask, "What does your Fourth of July mean to me?" Washington and Garvey wanted Black people to come to the table with some fruits of their labor. Both Washington and Garvey knew we needed and need, again in Margaret Walker's words, "something all our own." Why did Du Bois fight them? What an ironic twist of fate that Du Bois was the beneficiary of Garvey's dreams. That DuBois was the Renaissance man who spent his last days in Ghana, a Black independent nation, under a Black president. How ironic that Louis Sullivan and Clarence Thomas are beneficiaries of the struggles of the sixties.

"YOU BETTER THINK ... THINK ABOUT WHAT YOU'RE TRYING TO DO TO ME."
—A. FRANKLIN

I am an american Black. Period. The rest is of no particular interest to me. Afro-American, African-American, whatever. I am not a hyphenated American, regardless of how others define themselves. They can be Italian-Americans, Irish-Americans, Jewish-Americans, or whatever hyphens they would like to use. For me, the noun is Black; american is the adjective.

I do not fool myself often. I laugh about definitions because laughter is, well, so much more pleasant. I am not a particularly well person. I have lived too long with sick people to think I have escaped their malady. Every now and then, for one reason or another, someone will ask to interview me or talk with me or I will skim back through what has been said of my work just to, well, more or less see how I am progressing. I have always laughed at the critics saying I am bitter and full of hate. Nothing could be further from the truth. I am not envious or jealous either. I am just me. And I do have strong feelings about that. I do not and did not and most likely will not ever feel that I have to justify that. I do not have to be a role model, a good person, a credit to the race. When I look at Phillis Wheatley, Harriet Tubman, Monroe Trotter, Frederick Douglass, Sojourner Truth, Booker T. Washington, George Washington Carver, for that matter, W.E.B. Du Bois, James Weldon Johnson, Langston Hughes, Nella Larsen, James Baldwin, and I cannot possibly exhaust the list but, hey, Malcolm X, Elijah Muhammad, Martin Luther King, Sr. and Jr., just to name a few, the race has built up a big enough account for me to charge whatever I'd like. Doesn't Toni Morrison have a character named "Stamp Paid"? Perfect. Black America is well in advance of the Sunday school tithing of the folks with whom we live.

I had the great pleasure of meeting Anna Hedgeman when she visited Fisk University during, I think, my junior year. She was talking to honors history class about Frederick Douglass: "Every time I see that statue of Lincoln sitting below the Emancipation Proclamation, I want to

have a statue of Frederick Douglass standing behind him
guiding his hand." I could see that. Lincoln was an inter-
esting white man who did the right thing, finally, by free-
ing the slaves in the states where he had no power to
enforce his decree. But hey, why be so picky? He did it.
True. But not for me. Not for Cornelia Watson so that she
could birth John Brown Watson in freedom and he could
marry Louvenia Terrell and they could conceive Yolande
Watson and she could marry Gus Giovanni and they could
conceive me. No. Not for me. Lincoln didn't care about
Cornelia Watson. Nor conceptualize me. Near the end of
Song of Solomon, Morrison has Milkman finally review his
life, and he realizes that it is the women who wanted him
to live. Or, as the father in *Sounder* says to his son, "I beat
the *death* they had planned for me; I want you to beat the
life." Am I saying I'm glad we have President's Day in-
stead of Lincoln's Birthday and Washington's Birthday?
No. I like my holidays to have real names. But I also know
I don't owe these people any great affection or loyalty.
They do not love me or mine. That, by the way, means I
live in a narrow world. Well, maybe not so narrow. Maybe
a more accurate way of looking at it is that I will not have
my world nor my worth determined by people who mean
me ill. Unlike Du Bois and his latter-day children, I do not
measure my soul by the tape of the white world.

> "IT'S BEEN A LONG TIME COMING . . . BUT MY CHANGE
> IS GONNA COME."
> —S. COOKE

Like most people approaching their fiftieth birthday
(I was born in 1943), I have contemplated the meaning
of my people. I have wondered why we were chosen for
this great, cosmic experience. We were not the first slaves
in human history, nor were we even the first chattel. We

were, however, the first slaves who chose, after freedom, to live among our enslavers. That is about the only thing that gives me hope. If God could part the Red Sea for Moses, surely the Atlantic Ocean posed no unsolvable problem. I have contemplated what life must have been like around 1865 or so when freedom became a possibility. Why didn't we seek boats to take us to Haiti, which was already a free, Black republic? Why didn't we start great treks, not just a few wagon trains here and there, to the uncharged lands of this nation? What made us determined to fight it out essentially where we were? Some books tell us we loved enslavement . . . we didn't have to worry about our care or our duties. Some books say we didn't know where to go. Some books tell us we believed the promises of emancipation that we would be given forty acres and a mule. Mostly I think it was cosmic. The spirituals show us a people willing to "wait on the Lord." Though "sometimes I feel like a motherless child . . . a long way from home," though we knew "the rock cried out no hiding place," though we had the "Good News" that "I got a crown up in the Heavens," we "were there when they crucified my Lord." We were chosen to be a witness. Like Job in his patience, like Samson in his foolishness, "my soul is a witness . . . for my Lord." And without that faith there is no foundation for this nation. America may not be the best nation on earth, but it has conceived loftier ideals and dreamed higher dreams than any nation. America is a heterogeneous nation of many different peoples of different races, religions, and creeds. Should this experiment go forth and prosper, we will have offered humans a new way to look at life; should it fail, we will simply go the way of all failed civilizations. The spirituals teach us that the problem of the twentieth century is not the problem of the color line. The problem of the twentieth century is the problem of civilizing white people.

When I was a little girl, you could still buy things at the five-and-dime. You could buy those paddles with the ball attached that you would sit and whack for hours; you could buy jacks and pick-up-sticks. You could buy spin tops that you pulled a string around and the top would go spinning off. If your surface was rocky the top would falter and fall; if your tip had a nick, it would jump and fall; if your release of the string was not smooth, it would jerk and fall. If you wanted your top to spin the longest you did everything you could to get and keep things smooth.

> "YOU READ MY LETTER BABY . . . SURE MUST HAVE READ MY MIND."
>
> —B. ECKSTINE

The poet lights her fortieth cigarette. She will go over her limit as she opens a new pack. It is her favorite time of the day . . . when morning begins fusing itself into night, bringing that nether light to the sky. The poet recommends life. She likes the idea of the human experiment going forth. She knows her people are more than capable. The worst blows have been thrown and parried. This is only the cleanup. Perhaps, she thinks, she should treat herself to something wonderful. Fish. Fried fish. The poet remembers her grandmother's joy at fried fish and extra salt. Yes. And maybe a cold beer to salute her mother. Good job, Mommy. I'm here; not necessarily crazy; looking forward to tomorrow. No mother could do more. Maybe, the poet thinks, I'll buy a lottery ticket. The forty-first cigarette is lit. First thing in the morning. Fish and a lottery ticket. Hey . . . we're going to make it.

HIS NAME IS MALCOLM

First we hear the drums. There are all kinds of drums. The drums are being beaten with sticks and hands . . . there is an incessant rhythm. There is nothing on screen, but we hear the drumming. The screen lightens up . . . HARLEM: 1920. We see the feet . . . run-down heels of men's shoes . . . polished but obviously well worn . . . a woman's foot comes out of a medium heel . . . she rubs it as if her corns hurt . . . we see the white shoes of nurses . . . the flat shoes of the young women. Then we move the camera up just a little bit and see an ocean of cuffs . . . neat . . . clean . . . pressed, and we pan up to the hems of the skirts and dresses of the women. The camera moves into the sky . . . a beautiful shot of the skyline of New York looking down Central Park across to the skyscrapers . . . we pan back to the tops of the buildings of Harlem. People are sitting out, men in shirt-sleeves or undershirts, women dressed like housewives, children happy and excited by the upcoming parade. Maybe some birds flutter by, a pigeon or so, then we move to a great, colorful plumage. Feathers are

everywhere. The plumage is flung up and we recognize the headdress of Marcus Garvey. Garvey steps slowly to the front of the gathered people. His flag bearer hoists the Red, Black, and Green. Garvey looks to his left, then to his right. The drum major high-steps, blowing his whistle. He turns and the parade begins.

The camera is now at face level. We see hundreds, no, thousands of faces marching with Garvey. As the parade goes down Seventh Avenue, passing known Harlem landmarks, the background dissolves to Chicago, then to the Cincinnati train station, showing soldiers and civilians disembarking from trains, coming up stairs, passing a sign that says, "Gateway to the South." The drums are still insisting while we hear the feet in a parade cadence, but we now see rural America, people standing in fields looking north as if they hear something. We change background again and see Jamaica and people looking north. Garvey's voice is now being heard. The Red, Black, and Green with the lone Black star is oversized. The camera pans down on Garvey explaining the meaning of the flag. The crowd is animated, clapping, assenting to Garvey's words. "Africa for Africans . . . at home and abroad!" Garvey proclaims and the crowd cheers and cheers and cheers.

In an office room overlooking the parade two men are watching from the window. They are Black. One is Du Bois, the other is a James Weldon Johnson–type figure; older than Du Bois and less agitated about the parade. "That man is dangerous," says Du Bois. "All our efforts to claim manhood rights are going up in smoke." "Oh, William. I've been all over the world. Even you were just last year in Paris with your own Pan-African Congress. People want something of their own." "But this is our own," Du Bois insists. "We are Americans. We have got to make our stand here." "But the

*lynchings, the burnings, the people just can't take much more.
We've got to have something to offer them." "I agree," says
Du Bois, "but this Garvey is as bad as Booker T. Why would
we voluntarily segregate ourselves? That's half the problem.
We need to work to show that we are good citizens, that we
do have a valid culture, that we are men." "That, too, in
good time." But the Johnson figure looks back out the win-
dow. "That Garvey really can rouse a crowd, can't he? He
really has the people." Du Bois frowns. "He's in the way. We
will never be free with that nihilistic philosophy. He's a dan-
ger to our freedom."*

*Now the camera moves into a big office. A pug-looking
official in shirt sleeves is asking for the latest figures on the
parade. "I wish we could send those jigaboos back to Af-
rica," the J. Edgar Hoover figure says to no one in partic-
ular. "Garvey has over a million coloreds in this so-called
Back to Africa Movement. He needs to be stopped. The good
colored folks don't like it and neither does the president."
Hoover looks up to the three or four G-men standing around.
"He has to be stopped." End of scene.*

*Swirling snow is blowing. The streets have few people on them
and they are moving quickly. DETROIT: 1930. The camera
pans Depression Detroit, coming to rest in a small, indis-
tinct room while a voice is saying: "We must carry on the
great work. I have been sent to the Lost-Found Nation of
Islam in North America. I cannot stay long, but I am
anointing you to be my worldly representative." The camera
comes full face with Elijah Muhammad. "Robert Poole," the
voice commands, "are you ready to forsake your former life,
your former associates, your earthly family, your name, and
follow me?" "I am," he replies. "I now greet you, Elijah
Muhammad. You must carry my Word forward." We then*

see Elijah Muhammad meeting with a small group of men in a home; we see spring and Muhammad is standing, talking to a larger group; we see the white heat of summer and Elijah is going into jail talking with the men; when the colors of autumn come, Elijah has gathered a crew of men who are calling Him Messenger. End of scene.

We are now in a kitchen of a worker. The man is eating, the woman is serving him. There are many children around. The man is saying, "Louise, I know they think because they deported Mr. Garvey we will be silent. Well, Louise, I've been silent too long. I know I have to take Mr. Garvey's message to the Black Man. Did you hear about that lynching last week? It just won't stop until we stop it." The woman is tending to the children and trying to eat. She is loving but worried. "Earl, what about us? We've been burned out of one place. They won't quit until they kill you. Please think about the children." "Louise, what kind of life will they have if I'm not a man? What kind of life will they lead if I can't stand up?" Next we see Louise and seven youngsters huddled in a broken-down house. Louise has obviously left them for a better world. The children are trying to care for her, but it is obvious that they are not capable. A social worker comes and gently herds the children away. The younger ones are crying. The middle boy looks defiant. He is the last to leave the run-down shack. He pulls the door closed and there is a loud SLAM. We then hear another SLAM, and Elijah is seen, coming out of prison. Elijah looks back and we hear the third SLAM: Malcolm Little is behind bars. End of scene.

It is visiting day in the Charlestown prison. Malcolm Little is being visited by his brother, Roger, and his sister, Ella. Roger gives indication of being mentally delicate, as was his mother, but he is excited about what he has learned. He and Ella are telling Malcolm about "the true religion for Black people. Write Mr. Muhammad, Malcolm. Do this for me. I know I won't be with you long. I have dreams like Mamma used to have. I've been crying in my sleep. I know I'll feel like I've done my work if I can get you to know about this man. Mr. Muhammad offers us a way out. He was in jail himself, for refusing the draft. He won't let the devils tell him anything. You need to know about this." Malcolm looks at his sister, who is nodding her head yes. "Roger is right. We've found a peace I didn't know existed. After that thing with Daddy . . . and Mamma, well, Mamma couldn't take any more. . . . I never thought I'd have a family again. But the Nation has given me a family . . . and wants us to come to you. Do it for the family, Malcolm. You remember how Daddy was always talking about Garvey and nation building. This man, Mr. Muhammad, is building what Daddy wanted. Look into it, Malcolm." A prison guard walks by. The three look up. Roger says: "Everybody who's not dead is in prison. These books will help you come back to us." Malcolm takes the books and kisses his brother and sister good-bye. End of scene.

Now we see Malcolm working out. We see him in the "yard" walking with a book in his hand. We see him in his cell reading; we see him in the library copying words. He receives a letter with a Chicago postmark. Malcolm opens the letter and a dirty, much-used five-dollar bill falls out. Malcolm reaches for the bill. He is touched, pleased and smiling.

It is insulting to the Black community that we have to sit through almost an hour of gibberish to get to what Spike Lee has promised: Malcolm X. The only excuses for the opening of the movie have to be (1) to pad it out to "epic" length and (2) to get Spike Lee's face on screen. Perhaps some Americans aren't interested in the history of Black Nationalism and perhaps, even, some Americans think Malcolm X has to be "entertaining" in order to be a successful movie, but others of the Black community have kept Malcolm X alive for all these twenty-seven years not because we envision his dancing at the Savoy or kissing some white woman or robbing someone's home; there are thousands of people who do that and more every day, and we do not remember or honor them. We have kept Malcolm X alive in our hearts and our culture because he embodies our dreams of transformation and redemption. The story is strong enough to be told straight.

Malcolm X had to be a dream of Elijah Muhammad. Elijah was the brain of the Nation, but Malcolm X was the voice. When the two men first meet, Lee has Malcolm crying, but I can't accept that. As a Christian, if I met Christ, I would probably cry and He would probably touch me. Then I would ask: "Lord, what would you have me do?" Elijah Muhammad had to have charged Malcolm with a task. Malcolm needed to be shown performing it. There would be no task too humble for him. Cleaning the temple, serving that small band around Elijah, listening, learning. He would have to earn Mr. Muhammad's trust. Then Muhammad would have sent him out with a trusted minister. Again, Malcolm would have performed honorably. We need the scene when Elijah Muhammad calls Malcolm into his study and asks the others to leave. Muhammad tells Malcolm his dreams for Black people. He talks about his life in Georgia; about meeting Wallace Fard and how he was converted. He tells Malcolm about his own limitations, what with his asthma preventing him from being a great speaker and maybe even laughing about his height. He tells Malcolm how together they can build a nation; together they can galvanize the masses just as Garvey did. He asks Malcolm if he will follow him. Malcolm, like a knight of old, pledges his life and honor to Elijah Muhammad.

We need to see Malcolm X building a temple. A temple is a building made of people. We need to watch him recruit the Fruit of Islam (FOI). We need to see their drills, their workouts, their disciplines. We need to see others fall to the side and to understand how Malcolm, even though he has to put them out, holds out hope for them. When we finally get to the scene where Malcolm goes to the police station to inquire about a man beaten by the police, we need to see him put the FOI in motion. Each man calling another. We need to watch those men come from their homes, their jobs, stopping in the middle of their meals, putting their books down to answer the call. When Malcolm tells the police captain to look out the window, we need the camera to pan those faces: some mean, some scared, some excited but all holding themselves in check. We need to look at the shoes and the cuffs of their pants; we need the drums to start. After the man is taken to the hospital and the conflict is resolved, the policeman tells Malcolm to turn it off. Malcolm makes a physical gesture and the FOI march off. We need the drums, solemn and steady, to march them back home. Back at the temple we need to see some of the men celebrating their victory. Malcolm has to mount the podium to say there is no celebrating; they just did their job. We need to hear the mumbling that Malcolm is getting just like King: "... *next thing we know he'll be talking nonviolence.*" We need the laughter while Malcolm, who has overheard the remark, ponders the significance.

Slowly coming on screen is the brown grass of a field. The camera follows the grass over to a river. We hear the water running while the drums begin coming up. The camera shows an object that is unclear but bobbing. We see a big cotton-gin fan and attached to it the body of a boy. Over the drums we hear a woman's cry, "Emmett . . . oh, Emmett." It is his mother who is sorely distressed. We see the crowds passing a coffin in Chicago, and we pan down on the horribly mutilated face of Emmett Till.

Next we are in Money, Mississippi, in a courtroom. People are drinking RC Colas and fanning themselves. The judge is charging the jury: "I'm sure every drop of Anglo-Saxon blood in you will give you the courage to free these men." The jury foreman returns the verdict: not guilty. We see the mother of Emmett Till saying: "I'm disappointed but I'm not surprised." We take a close look at the face of Mrs. Bradley; the camera holds it until it dissolves into the face of Rosa Parks saying, "Why do you all push us around?" She is sitting on a bus and refusing to move. The bus driver is asking her, almost pleading: "Make it easy on yourself and give me those seats." Mrs. Parks sits: "No." We see footage of King giving the first charge to the Montgomery boycott. We see people running off flyers and distributing them. The buses roll on Monday and they are empty. We see the arrest of King and the booking, the photographing, the fingerprinting. We see King's home being bombed and King addressing the crowd, telling them to go home. We see Martin Luther King, Jr., walk to a desk drawer and take out a handgun. He walks to the back of his house and throws it away in his garbage can. King is speaking to Ralph Abernathy: "Ralph, we can't win this one with guns. If they have an excuse to kill us all, they will. We have to find another way." Now we see King picking up the books. He is reading about Gandhi. We

*see King at the closing rally after the boycott is won. King is
holding up the papers on the Supreme Court ruling. He gives
the speech on redemptive love. We cut back to Malcolm, who
is giving a speech in the temple about the foolishness of loving
your enemy. Malcolm is saying Muslims don't turn the other
cheek. The camera turns to a church bombing; four girls are
killed Sunday morning in church. King is saying we will
stay in Birmingham; Malcolm X is saying we don't want to
integrate with that pale ol' thing. We see the police dogs
being sicced on the protesters; the camera cuts back to Mal-
colm saying: "Kill the dog! I say if they dogs attack us . . . kill
the dogs."*

Both young Black men were contending for the soul of
Black America. White America had considered King radi-
cal until Malcolm's voice began to be heard. Our movie
should show books and articles being written about the
Black Muslims, television shows being produced. People
are listening to Malcolm X and this, quite naturally, is
causing some problems with the ministry in Chicago.

*Cut to Chicago. A few ministers, maybe three, are saying to
Elijah Muhammad that Malcolm is getting too big. Mr.
Muhammad tells them to look around. Look at the number
of temples that have been built; look at the membership and
how it has grown. This is due to Malcolm. He assures them
that Malcolm enjoys his highest confidence. In fact, he is
sending for Malcolm and they will talk. He will have no
more of this dissension.*

*Malcolm and the Messenger are talking in Mr. Muham-
mad's den. A very pretty, pregnant woman is bringing coffee
or tea to both men. Malcolm is asking Mr. Muhammad if
this is a wise move. What will their enemies say if they find*

out Malcolm is meeting with these men. "Malcolm," Mr.
Muhammad says patiently, "look at our people. They are
poor, hungry, in jail, or just out. Without money we can't
help them. Look at our schools, our businesses, our newspaper,
our restaurants. Do you think we can continue these things
without money? Where will we get it? Do you think the
government is going to give us a grant? None of these devils
like us. Not the liberal devils; not the reactionary devils. They
are all racists. We have to take the money where we can."
Malcolm is shaking his head in agreement, but there is puz-
zlement on his face. "Messenger, I have pledged my life to
you. I will always do as you ask. I just hate to think that we
are giving a weapon to our enemies." "I'll do the thinking,
Malcolm. I'll do the thinking for the Lost-Found Nation in
North America." The woman moves some things from Mr.
Muhammad's desk. She is fussing over him. Malcolm looks at
her with questions in his eyes. He rises, goes to get his coat.
"Good night, sir. I'll be leaving early in the morning before
you awake." Mr. Muhammad absently waves Malcolm
away. End of scene.

We see the skyline of New Orleans and two men, one Mal-
colm X, one white but obviously underworld. They are walk-
ing through the French Quarter. They are talking but we
cannot hear their words. There is the faint sound of drums.
The white man passes something to Malcolm, who takes it
and turns a corner. We see the Gateway Arch of St. Louis.
Malcolm is watching the Mississippi flow when a long lim-
ousine, black, pulls up and a white man emerges. The sounds
of the river give way to the sounds of the drums. The white
man hands something to Malcolm X and walks back to the
car. We see the plane landing in Denver. Malcolm rents a
car and drives into the country. He emerges after a long

drive at a lodge. There are several white men to greet him. The drums are humming in the background. "Look around," one of the men tells Malcolm. "This is what your people need; some private place to train. Nothing but the best here." They take Malcolm inside. They all sit around the fireplace. "Give my regards to the Messenger," says one man. "He is the only colored person in America who knows up from down." Malcolm is clearly uncomfortable with these men. "That King, Martin Luther Coon"—they all laugh— "is causing all this trouble. Kennedy can't control him. Something's gonna have to be done soon. Now you people . . . you don't want to vote, you don't want our jobs, you don't want anything from America. That's a program we can get behind." They are all laughing and talking. Malcolm is very quiet. Someone announces that dinner is served. They all move to the table. There is ham and fried chicken. Malcolm has a cup of coffee, "Black," he says. "Strong." They all laugh again. Malcolm is readying to go. The first white man puts a briefcase in Malcolm's hands. "Now see to it this gets directly to the Messenger, boy," the white man says with no particular inflection. It is his way of talking. Malcolm looks at him strangely and smiles. "Yes, sir," Malcolm says with a broad grin. "I certainly will."

Malcolm is on a plane to Chicago. He is looking out the window and it becomes spring. He sees Betty Sanders in the audience. They meet. He begins to look forward to seeing her. He calls her one day and asks her to marry him. She says yes without hesitation. We see Malcolm deliver the briefcase to Mr. Muhammad. He is anxious to get home to New York. Mr. Muhammad is asking if he needs a larger house, now that the baby has come. Does he need a new car? Is everything all right? Malcolm assures Mr. Muhammad that everything is fine. He is simply anxious to get home to Betty and Attilah.

Mr. Muhammad hugs Malcolm with a puzzled look on his face. Malcolm embraces Mr. Muhammad with distaste. The woman Malcolm had seen earlier is still around, fussing after the Messenger. End of scene.

I obviously am not a movie maker. I just wanted to see for myself if I could at least construct a better film than that sick joke Spike Lee entitled *Malcolm X*. I went to the theater wanting very much to like the movie. A source I have highest respect for said, "Well, you won't be embarrassed." But I am. Had I possessed a piece of rotten fruit, I would have hurled it at the screen. What was the purpose of Spike Lee's being the first face on screen? Why did Malcolm look like a country bumpkin waiting in the barber shop? Where did that doofus Malcolm come from? Why were Spike and Malcolm the only people in zoot suits, making them look like clowns? Why didn't Denzel Washington ever stand up straight for the first, laborious hour of the film? I think it's more than fair to say Spike Lee hates Black women. What was the purpose of having that white man pick up that Black woman, take her into an alley à la *Catch-22* and have her go down on him? What narrative drive was served by her humiliation? And I totally fail to understand why Denzel, being in bed with a woman whom he wants to humiliate, tells her to kiss his foot. Men have asked women to kiss many things, and "foot" has got to be the last of them. Spike chose the Black woman going down on the white man to "put her in her place" but did not dare risk showing a white woman doing the same thing to a Black man. As a Black woman, I grow ever more disturbed by Spike Lee.

In *She's Gotta Have It*, the young Black woman was attacked; in *School Daze,* Black institutions from the schools to the fraternities are attacked; *Mo' Better Blues* gave us a doofus musician who didn't know one woman from another and stupidly mounted the stage to play without ever realizing his lips had been permanently damaged; *Jungle Fever* is a case study in sexual harassment. Why couldn't he find a woman who was his equal? And all that talk from Spike about how he doesn't believe in interracial sex is disingenuous at best. What movie has Spike Lee ever made that David Duke, now that his bid for higher office is only a distant dream, couldn't make? *Do the Right Thing?* Spike, playing another diminutive male, working in a pizza parlor on the hottest day of the year, gives us an overworked song coming too loud from a radio and murmurs from the Black community as the police kill Radio Raheem. Don't let me forget we also get the longest *yooooooooooooo* in the history of the world, but mostly, what happens to the neighborhood? Where are the people? What are the antecedents? We get stereotypical whites and stereotypical Blacks and signs—there are always signs in Spike Lee's movies, trying to explain what the movie couldn't.

Lee was not the director or writer for Malcolm. It is not X and that was not his name. His name was Malcolm. And whether he was rebelling against a teacher who tried to "put him in his place" or a system that tried to "put him in his place" or a religion that tried to "put him in his place," he fought for his individual dignity as a Black man. He picked up and put down many weapons in that struggle: nihilism, crime, withdrawal, belief in Elijah, belief in Allah, belief in himself, but he always fought. Malcolm X was an angry man. Malcolm Little and El Hajj Malik El-Shabazz was an angry man. If you liked him at the end, you liked him at the beginning. His goals were not always clear, and the ending, being what it was, does not speak to him ever being a "good boy." King, who certainly, and for no reason, got the brunt of Lee's venom, was a "good, Christian man" who was shot down, just as Malcolm, the rude boy, was. Both men gave their lives for the dignity and integrity of Black people. If Malcolm moved to "some white people are not devils," King moved to "some white brothers are sick." Did Elijah order Malcolm assassinated? Given the climate and infiltration of that time, he didn't have to. Neither did J. Edgar Hoover. All anyone had to do was restrict Malcolm's movements and incite some of the less stable young men. We see it today. When the Black community claims the white community is waging war against us, the white community replies, "You are killing yourself." Yet the young men in the streets neither make nor import the drugs or guns. Somebody is bringing them in. Would I like to see it stopped? You bet. But it takes more than good intentions. Elijah may have had his faults. I am not and have not been a Muslim, yet we all must concede that Elijah offered a program and a hope that has yet to be repeated. He was not some sickly, jealous man who coughed his godfatherly way into the Black community. He was a giant; a nation builder who, in Malcolm, found the voice he needed. You have to show Elijah as more than a delicate old fool. Were there jealousies in the Nation? Certainly! As there were jealousies in the civil rights movement. As Bush, in fact, hates Clinton, and Truman refused to ride with Ike. It is not unusual, in fact it would be extremely rare, if differences were not there. But the job of the storyteller, who is weaving the saga of his people, is to tell us why they were heroes; what they overcame in both the outside world and within themselves.

I hated the ending. If all it took to be Malcolm X is a doofus schoolteacher saying something and some doofus children standing up, then we would have another Malcolm X and another. Twenty-eight years would not have gone by without several other Malcolms coming along. If Lee wanted to show Malcolm's impact in Africa, he needed to show Malcolm addressing the Organization of African Unity on his trip home from Mecca. Lee needed to show African leaders from Egypt to Ghana receiving Malcolm as a head of state. And whatever happened to Cassius Clay? One of the main reasons he became an international figure, beloved the world over, was his conversion to Muhammad Ali, a conversion wrought by Malcolm's influence. Malcolm made an impact on the world. Yet where, in Spike Lee's film, do we see his greatness?

Lee has a marked inability to show historical antecedents. He is only good at attacking those parts of the Black community that we hold dear: the Black woman; our schools; our music; our neighborhoods; our families; our shining Black princes. This son of Clarence Thomas, this revisionist, this man who is not short in height so much as small in stature, needs to hear one of his own symbols: the bell in *School Daze*. Malcolm X was assassinated by Black men in 1965; but he is being destroyed in 1993 by stupidity and greed. The question about Malcolm's death is also the question about Lee's movie: Who gave the order? Whose interests were served in each case? Wake up, Lee. The drums are calling.

SHOOTING FOR THE MOON

> I WAS BORN IN THE CONGO
> I WALKED TO THE FERTILE CRESCENT AND BUILT THE
>   SPHINX
> I DESIGNED A PYRAMID SO TOUGH THAT A STAR THAT
>   ONLY GLOWS EVERY ONE HUNDRED YEARS FALLS
>   INTO THE CENTER GIVING DIVINE PERFECT LIGHT
> I AM BAD . . .
> I MEAN . . . I . . . CAN FLY
>   LIKE A BIRD IN THE SKY . . .

I wrote that poem, "Ego Tripping," over twenty years ago. And now, I'm so proud that on September 12, 1992, Dr. Mae Carol Jemison made history by flying *higher* than any bird in the sky. As the first Black woman astronaut, she rode the shuttle *Endeavor* into the space around the earth as a science mission specialist.

I'm a space nut. I remember thinking when *Sputnik I* took off in 1957 that now "we are earthlings." I've also been a Trekkie since the television series *Star Trek* began. I was intrigued that a sister, Nichelle Nichols, was Uhura, the communications officer. It was so right, it made such sense that the voice of the Federation would be the voice of a Black woman. Toni Morrison says, in *Tar Baby,* "The Black woman is both a ship and a safe harbor." Lieutenant Uhura proved that. So, while I was glad to see America's first woman astronaut, Sally Ride, go above the atmosphere, I knew what was actually needed was a Black woman: Mae C. Jemison.

I am at breakfast with Mae Jemison. I am, naturally, nervous. I am a middle-aged, cigarette-smoking, unhealthy and uninterested-in-health poet who has just snagged the opportunity of a lifetime. I get to interview Mae Jemison.

I would have liked her even if she hadn't said my smoking wouldn't bother her; I would have liked her even if she hadn't said, "Oh, I didn't get straight A's in school like my sister," with a devilish smile, "because I took subjects I was interested in." I would have liked her had she been arrogant and impatient with a poet whose view of space is metaphysical, not physical, but she was not only patient but kind.

"Aren't you bored a lot?" I was compelled to ask. I mean, she sits talking to people who haven't a hoot in hell what she actually does or can do. "A friend once told me: 'If you are bored, you're not paying attention.' I think he's right."

Over breakfast, Mae told me this story: "When I came home for Christmas, my first year at Stanford University, I had brought my calculus with me. My mother said, 'Why don't you ask your father to help you?' I thought she couldn't be serious. My father is a high school graduate, and I was this, well, hotshot at Stanford. But I did ask him for help, and he made it so clear to me. That one thing changed the way I thought about my father and myself."

There is something about Alabama men and numbers. My father, like hers, was a mathematical whiz, and like hers, was from a little city outside Mobile. My mother, like Mae's, also taught school. But I grew up in Cincinnati, and Mae's hometown is Chicago.

"You know what my mother told me one day?" Mae asked. "I was feeling really good about some project I had finished, and she just sort of looked at me and said, 'But you're illiterate.' I was crushed. How could my mother consider me illiterate?'' Mae laughs and shakes her head. She was so upset that she set out to learn more about Black literature and history. Her undergraduate double degree at Stanford was in chemical engineering and African and African-American studies. "But what made you decide to go to medical school after undergraduate?" I asked her. "Well," she ponders, "I could have gone into dance, which I love, or I could have gone to medical school. I just chose medical school." There is something wonderful about the way Mae phrases her choices. They are, well, logical. She doesn't feel special, just prepared to control her options.

Opting against a traditional career in medicine, Mae joined the U.S. Peace Corps as a medical officer in Sierra Leone and Liberia. I asked her if this has had any effect on her desire to serve others. Intriguingly enough, she bristled: "I don't believe in altruism. I've gotten much more out of what I have done than the people I was supposed to be helping. When I was in the refugee camp in Thailand, I learned more about medicine there than I could have in a lifetime somewhere else. I refuse to think those people owe me any thanks. I got a lot out of it."

After leaving the Peace Corps, she was a general practitioner and attending graduate engineering classes in Los Angeles when she was tapped by NASA in 1985. There have been four other Black women astronauts in training with her, but now she is the only one. Until her next flight, which is unscheduled, Mae spends her work days earthbound at NASA in Houston doing scientific experiments.

I'm the original little girl who wouldn't take biology because you had to cut up a frog. "Tell me," I bravely asked, "about your frog experiment." "We wanted to know,"

Jemison said, "how the tadpoles would develop in space, with no gravity. I hatched the eggs and developed the tadpoles. They showed no ill effects, and since frogs, like other life forms, take so much of their basic knowledge from their environment, we were curious if they would hear well, if they would turn out to be . . . well, normal frogs. When we got back to earth, the tadpoles were right on track and they have turned into frogs." Now I got to ask an intelligent question: "If most of the learning of, for example, frogs is genetic, then won't it be the second generation which will show the effects of the trip, not the first? If, in other words, there is a mutation taking place, won't we have to wait at least until the next generation before we see the effects?" But what I—and I suspect, she—was most interested in is, How can space technology help us? If the second-generation frog shows some mutation that is the result of the stress of being born in space, what will this tell us about the second generation being born in, for example, slavery or the second generation that is homeless or the fifth generation being born into a racist world? Will the mutations be aberrant, or will they be the logical adjustment to a foreign, untoward pressure? And can we ever be the same once such a change has taken place?

"What are your thoughts when you're whirling in space?"

"The first thing I saw was Chicago. I looked out the window and there it was," she says, and adds that she also saw all of earth. "I looked over at one point and there was Somalia." She was in space while others were in the last throes of starvation.

"Space is so meaningful to earth," Jemison says. "The third world will be the ultimate beneficiary of space technology because we're moving away from infrastructures.

You don't need to lay telephone wire to have phones anymore; that's what cellular is all about. We don't need old-fashioned generators for electrical connections anymore. The third world will be able to jump over the industrial age into the space age." It surprises Jemison that there aren't more Afrocentric people excited about space and its technology.

"You know what I took with me when I went up?" I did know, but I let her say it. "An Alvin Ailey American Dance Theater company poster, an Alpha Kappa Alpha banner, a flag that had flown over the Organization of African Unity, and proclamations from Chicago's Du Sable Museum of African-American History and the Chicago public school system. I wanted everyone to know that space belongs to all of us. There is science in dance, and art in science. It belongs to everyone. I'm not the first or the only African-American woman who had the skills and talent to become an astronaut. I had the opportunity. All people have produced scientists and astronomers." And though she bristles at altruisms, clearly all her interests are of service to humankind.

Was she afraid? "You are aware that you're on a controlled explosion; but I have confidence in NASA." Plus, you have to think whatever Mae Jemison knows about fear was left in her mother's kitchen.

Mae Jemison is a mind in motion. If that devilish grin and those piercing eyes could be stripped away, I think you would find pure energy in constant motion. We use *genius* very lightly. In the movie *Sneakers,* the geek had a license plate that said 180IQ; I knew Debi Thomas would not prevail when I saw that her license plate said SKATING FOR GOLD. It was too much pressure. Mae Jemison is enjoying her life and its opportunities. Single, thirty-six, and living in the home she bought in suburban Houston, she loves the music of Etta James, and she talks as easily to children as to scientists. She's comfortable with herself.

What's next? If she could design her ideal space trip, what would it be? Her answer: "Me in a clear bubble floating through the galaxy . . . shooting for the moon." Who would she want to go with her? "Sneeze, my cat. I think I'd like to have Sneeze. He came with me from Africa, so he's used to flying. Then," that grin again, "if some aliens came by and invited me to another galaxy— well, look for me on *Unsolved Mysteries*. I'm gone."

III

"WIND IN THE COTTON FIELDS"

—LANGSTON HUGHES

ANNUAL CONVENTIONS OF EVERYDAY SUBJECTS

"... FROM AMONG TEN THOUSAND WOMEN TO MAKE
A FIVE-MINUTE PRESENTATION IN NEW YORK ON ..."

The poet had decided to accept the invitation to address the 372nd Annual Convention of Black and White Women in America. Sure, she'd be misunderstood by both parties, vilified and lied on by one; venerated and quoted by the other . . . but hey . . . what's life without a little spice? And who's to say which side would do what? The poet was, in essence, a gameswoman . . . raunchy even . . . but the world is a game . . . deep and dirty. The poet knew all about games. She had studied the men. The Princeton men, the Yale men, the Marshall men, the technical men; the men with stomachs of jelly and backbones to match. The erected men who protested abortions, the religious men who sniffed women's panties, the athletic men whose balls weren't always on the field, yes . . . she would talk to the women of these men because it was all so . . . well . . . silly. The women fight over these men and who gets to service them. Mothers fighting with wives over who cooks for the sons, wives fighting with mistresses over whose children are legitimate, every one of them trying to stay thin and young so the men will enjoy looking at them. Each one of them determined to infantilize the men to keep her place assured. It is all so illogical . . . stupid childish game . . . grown women unsure of their place in his heart.

As the poet began to prepare her remarks, she felt glad that she is a Black woman. She remembered her mother's friends. The women, Flora and Theresa, who would take time to listen to her, though what no child says makes sense. The women who would pay and praise her for cleaning their stoves and refrigerators, letting her know her work was valuable. The women who would exclaim . . . yes, exclaim . . . over how wonderful her hair looked when braided. The women who would counsel her on which sorority she should join when . . . not if . . . she went to college. The women who had plans for her. The poet contemplated her grandmother and her friends. How at church on Sundays they would ask about and expect a report on her grades. How her grandmother would give her books the book club was reading so that the grandmother and she could discuss them before Grandmother was due to make her report. How Grandmother would stop and listen to what the poet said, though in retrospect, the poet knows she brought no insight. Ahhh, the beauty of the games of Black women. They make you feel smart and courageous and brave. The poet contemplated her mother: four feet, eleven inches. The poet was an old woman before she realized her five feet, two inches, in the real world, wasn't tall.

Being a woman of education, the poet knew that in order to properly approach any subject, research is necessary. She went to her library, which was composed of the books bequeathed or given to her from the libraries of her grandfather, grandmother, and parents. She browsed the section containing great speeches: Frederick Douglass, Sojourner Truth, Mary Church Terrell, W.E.B. Du Bois, Marcus Garvey, Ella Baker, Rosa Parks, Martin Luther King, Jr., and Sr. No. Nothing sufficient on white women. She browsed sociology; political science. Sure, there had been great white women but they were exceptional. In law, there is an expression: "Hard cases make bad law." In life, exceptional people make poor generalizations. A white person could befriend, even love, a Black person and never change his/her attitude about Black people. A Black person will witness horrors and take a passing friendship with a white person to show "not all of them are like that." It's so . . . well . . . Christian . . . to hate the deed yet love the doer. The poet called the white women she knew . . . all three of them. "I have been invited to address the 372nd Annual Convention of Black and White Women in America," she told them. "This may be my only chance to reach this many people. What should I say?" She sighed. "Would it be fair to bring up the, well, hurt we felt when you spit on our children trying to desegregate schools? Or is the fifties too long ago? I guess I shouldn't mention the women in the lynch mobs as Black men, hands tied behind their backs, were hanging from trees. I suppose we shouldn't even talk about how the women's movement wouldn't listen to the Black women when we tried to say that the average white woman didn't understand her maid. I mean, when Lana Turner said to Annie, 'I didn't know you belonged to a lodge,' Juanita Moore replied, 'Well, Miss Laura, you never asked.' There was no *women's* movement; there was a *white* women's movement and Black women never were, nor felt, included. It's all been an *imitation of life* to us and *the long walk home* won't change that. Should I mention," the poet continued, "that we get tired of your impatience? That snappy white-girl way you have of saying something to us? That . . . well . . . debutante way you have of thinking what you have said is significant and important and must be responded to right away? Or is that too petty?"

The poet wondered if she should even consider mentioning how very tired she is, personally, of white women telling her what Black women are really like. And should she demur, those women going on to explain how the book they recently read stated a different reality. Should she say how tired she is of issues being "women" until it is a Black woman and then that very same issue becoming one of qualifications and philosophy? From the glass ceilings of business to the straw floors of academia there is always a reason not to pay or promote a Black woman. Should the poet say how tired Black women are of being used? How upsetting it was to us that Tawana Brawley, a minor who is Black and made a rape charge against white men, had her name, address, and photograph in every major news publication, while we had to watch a national television news program blue-dot the face of a grown white woman who picked up a man in a bar, drove him to his house, got out of the car with him, watched him undress and go for a swim, waited until he came out of the ocean naked and ready for sex, and then was protected from undue publicity? Should I even deign to mention the Scottsboro Boys or Emmett Till? Dare I ask how does it feel to have a horrible crime committed in your name?

But hey . . . maybe I should just stick to the basics.

My friends suggested that I at least mention some things I like about white women. No problem. I like frontier women. Maybe I've been overly influenced by *Little House on the Prairie,* but I think it awfully brave that a woman, with her children, would go into the tall grass among natives who had reason to be very unfriendly, with a man she barely knew who had a dream of making his life better. Frontier man tried to conquer the wilderness; frontier woman tried to tame it. I like the white women who came south after the Civil War to man (woman?) the freedman's normal schools and colleges. And I like the white women who stood with us in the sixties. It's been a little disappointing in the eighties and nineties to watch the affirmative action men and white women turn in their love beads for brown shirts, turning their backs on the people's movement that made their positions possible, but hey . . . this is, I suppose, the real world. "Well," the poet's friends pointed out, "you don't want to be a downer. Say something funny. Give white women a challenge and a charge. But be yourself." The poet decided to take that advice.

Wanting to make a positive impression, though recognizing Black success opens no doors just as Black failure closes none, the poet had her long, blue skirt and white-with-pin-striped-blue blouse cleaned. On the occasion of her sister's graduation from college, the poet and she had gone to Paris. They had purchased two ties for their father that, after his death, the poet had had cut down to woman-size for each of them. The poet is not only sentimental; she needed the strength. Reaching for her wild winterberry lipstick, the poet made ready to face the podium. Her speech:

OK. I think it's important to admit, up front, that we

*don't always ... well ... get along. I know it grabs my
very last nerve to be at any and all public events and have
the blonde in front of me either fluff out her hair or ac-
tually ... start to comb it. I brush and brush madly at
unseen cooties on my skirt, my blouse, my blue jeans even
because ... well ... there must have been some reason she
started to comb her hair in the first place. Was it something
living? Was it some itch indicating an infection? Some vi-
ral life form that will now come to my seat? Why on earth
do white women comb their hair in public? It's bad enough
in the bathroom where they hog the mirrors. All I want,
honestly, is a little peek at my face, but I'm afraid ...
really, I am ... to step into the jangle of blond, red, bru-
nette, and whatever living color is flying around there.
Then they leave all that hair in the sink. Maybe, OK, ac-
tually, I'm compulsive. I was always taught never to leave
hair in the bathroom sink ... not even my own. I'll even
grant that the reason is our plumbing wasn't good. What-
ever reason you may wish to ascribe is fine but ...* I hate
hair in a sink! *It doesn't just look unclean, which it is, but
unhealthy. Admit it. You've never used a sink in a public
place after a Black woman and seen hair. Maybe you are
getting ready to say "Well, gee! You people hardly have
enough hair to leave." But that's not true. I can uncurl a
very long strand if I want, and I wear an Afro. We have
the hair; it just curls next to our head. You could say it's
well trained: It stays where it was originally put.*

    And speaking of originally put, the poet neatly segued
à la Marlin Perkins of *Wild Kingdom* fame, *you and I were
originally put on earth for the purpose of furthering human
life. We were originally put here to help each other and be a
caretaker for those unable to care for themselves. Our orig-
inal purpose was noble and proper. If Steven Spielberg can*

take up Back to the Future, *you and I can go forward to the past. Human beings need each other. That is an honorable calling. I hope we can heed it.*

The poet was finished. She lit a cigarette. She had done today's job today. She asks no more of herself.

PIONEERS: A GUIDE

The first pioneers who were Black came to America as explorers. Though exploring is a pioneering adventure, they were simply considered men who sailed toward the unknown, seeking riches, dreams . . . something different. History has ignored them, tried to wipe them out, because the people who could have told their story didn't realize there was a story to tell.

The Africans who came to this shore from the second decade of the seventeenth century weren't considered pioneers either. No one sang songs of their journey, no one would be on shore to welcome them home. They came in chains on ships that would never take them back. "I'm going to fly away . . . one of these days . . . I'm going to fly away." They were the true pioneers. We talk, in American history, about the wagons moving westward, but we don't get the miniseries of *Middle Passage;* we get no weekly sitcom called "My Night in the Galley." The songs that were ultimately sung were sung by us about us. But the true pioneers were those whose hearts, hands, and souls made this land come alive. Black pioneers cultivated the land and Black songs cultivated the spirit.

You would think from our history books that Frederick Douglass and Harriet Tubman were just about the only Black people who were abolitionists, all other people of color being so very content just to be a slave or to be some sort of "freed man." I don't think so. The slaves who had to stay and the slaves who were able to leave were pioneers not only of Black freedom but of the American ideal.

The Harlem Renaissance brought us another pioneer, artistic pioneers. For the first time, the masses of people could not only create something but sign their names to it. It could be a poem, a play, a novel, a dance, a piece of music or sculpture, or the food on the table. In the 1920s, for the first time, a "signature" was meaningful to Blacks because we owned ourselves.

Throughout these centuries Black Americans have been breaking open doors that others would close, opening lands others stumbled through, finding emotional strength to carry on when a lesser people would have capitulated. Emmett Till found the strength to put his socks on before he was carried out to be brutally murdered; his mother found the strength to open his casket. Rosa Parks found the strength to stay seated; Martin Luther King found the words to define a movement.

But if there has been one overwhelming effort made by Blacks since the beginning of our American sojourn, it has been the belief in the need to obtain education. The laws that were made against our reading, voting, holding certain jobs, living in certain areas, were made not because we were incapable; you don't have to legislate against incapability. No one tells an infant, "You can't walk"; one tells that to a toddler. No one tells a six-year-old, "You can't drive"; one tells that to a fifteen-year-old. No one tells a man or a woman, "You can't read," unless there is the knowledge that if that person becomes educated, he or she will no longer be my slave; will no longer sharecrop my land; will no longer tolerate injustice.

Those of you looking now at colleges are pioneers, too. History may not record your struggles, but they will be there, and you, like your ancestors, will have to find a way to overcome. Education, higher education, graduate education, professional school—all these different ways of learning more and more will set you more and more alone . . . will make you stand out and become a target. But as you climb the education ladder, your ancestors hope you will "walk together, Children . . . and don't you get weary." Every pioneer looks at a horizon, and sometimes that horizon can look so far that it seems safer and easier to go back. Your ancestors are whispering: "Don't let nobody turn you 'round." College is a great, though difficult, adventure. Those of you who find your way there, like our ancestors on stormy seas, like our foreparents forging their way on the underground railroad, like your grandparents working against legal segregation, like your parents sitting in, kneeling in, praying in in the sixties, know that once again Black Americans are being called to be our best selves. Knowledge is power. May that force be with you.

THIS HAS NOTHING TO DO WITH YOU: A SPECIAL MESSAGE TO AFRICAN-AMERICAN COLLEGIANS

There is a photograph that I hung in my son's room. It shows a Black man, clearly emancipated . . . not a slave, standing behind a mule. In his right hand he is holding the plow; in his left he has a McGuffey *Reader.* I wanted that picture in my son's room because I wanted him to know, viscerally, who he is and where he comes from. I don't know that the picture made all that much difference to Tom. He would probably have preferred some busty woman in some lewd or obscene pose, but since I am grown and he wasn't, I won the first battle of the walls.

The need to read and write is genetically deep. Humans have drawn on cave walls, fashioned language from the animal and natural sounds surrounding us. The need to communicate is basic to humans. Education is still the key.

I would not be so naive as to say or think that without formal education people cannot survive or thrive. Black people, especially, have done both. When we were, as a group, forbidden to read and write, when our drums were taken from us, when our religious practices were forbidden, we couched our tales in the spirituals, saying, "Go down, Moses" when Harriet Tubman and the underground railroad were ready to roll; we sang "Steal Away" when we were going to run; we released our sorrow in "Nobody knows the trouble I've seen"; and we shouted our Good News in "I've got a crown up in the Heavens . . . ain't that Good News." No history course can tell me the slaves didn't leave a record. They sang, "Deep River . . . my home is over Jordan." They told us, "You got to walk this lonesome valley." They told us, "Wade in the water . . . God's gonna trouble the water." The slaves left a record; America just doesn't like the fact that "everybody talking 'bout Heaven ain't going there."

I guess I just don't understand why this generation is so lost. The young people who are dropping out of school could not understand the fight of our people for literacy. Could not understand that one of the main reasons you could get "sold south" was because you could read and write. The young people today must never have sat and read the Constitution, let alone the *Federalist Papers,* or they would surely know how essential the Black presence in the New World was. It's not just that Blacks supplied labor; we supplied the skills that made that labor necessary. What did Europeans know about planting? What did they know about iron and bronze? Only what we taught them. Who has pondered the illogicality of bringing women to the New World? Slavery had existed and still does exist on earth. No people in their right mind would bring a woman across the seas. The Romans never thought to bring Greek women. Look at slavery in the African continent. You killed and enslaved the men. The women you left behind. Why? Because once you bring the female, you cannot breed the Black out. Look at the Moors in Spain, look at France, Germany, England. Look at Switzerland today with its "Turkish" problem and at what was once West Germany for the same situation. Why did they bring women to America? It's a question needing an answer.

But what has this got to do with you? If you knew that Liberia was founded in 1822 to send free and emancipated Blacks there, what does it mean that some stayed because they wanted to and others stayed because they had to? The solution was in the hands of the Americans. Why didn't they take it? How can anyone say the Civil War was not fought over slaves? Of course it was. Free labor cannot compete with slave labor. But why would poor white boys fight for a system that does not benefit them? Perhaps for the same reason Black men fought the Indians with the British, defeating the Black men who fought the Indians with the French. How can you be a Black man and not understand the great job the Black preacher did in getting the slaves one day off? I still hear people saying the preacher is nothing. Where is their sense of history? How would they like to be alive in 1750 or so, trying to convince a planter that on a pretty day, which just happens to be a Sunday, the slaves should be allowed to praise God? What kind of network would we have had without the preacher? What would have happened to our language if the preacher had not been allowed to study the Bible? How would our story have been kept alive if we had not found a song in code?

All I'm saying is this stuff today has nothing to do with us. The drugs, the drive-by shootings, the pregnancies, the dropouts . . . these are not us. We have come through the fires. How can we now be tired? Isn't there an old song that says, "Walk together, children, don't you get weary"?

And didn't we sing that in Montgomery, Selma, and all over the South? Why did we do that? For a cup of coffee? For the joy of voting for Lyndon Johnson over Barry Goldwater? We did it for the future. Why now, young Black men, have you decided to live in the present? What happened to the future vision of your grandfathers and great-grandfathers? Why now do you have to go to jail before you take time to commune with yourselves? Why do you have to be on death row before you decide to read a book or study law or heroically save someone's life? Your generation talks a lot about "roles." What "role" will you play in life? Try man. Try responsible man. Try forward-looking man. Try man who learns something the easy way (college) instead of the hard way (prison). Try doing the very difficult job of helping yourself and someone else by building something. Try honoring the very best in yourself instead of the very worst.

Am I picking on the men? I hope not. I hope I am reminding you that you have a job to do today. I hope I am reminding you that the people who produced you had little reason to dream; yet dream they did. They dreamed that one day you would be judged by the content of your character. They had no doubt that you would pass the test. Something has got to turn around.

Clearly the men are going to have to change. Malcolm X was fond of saying, "Show me how a country treats its women, and I'll show you the progress of that nation." We in Black America have turned that around: Show me how men treat each other, and I will show you the future of those people.

Those of you, young African-American men, who are struggling in high school and college . . . you are our pioneers. Don't let people tell you it is "individualistic" to try to do something with your life. Frederick Douglass was "individualistic" when he walked off that plantation in Maryland; David Walker was "individualistic" when he wrote his appeal; Marcus Garvey was "individualistic" when he got on that boat in Jamaica and came to America, and the people he organized were "individualistic" in their desire to make a better life. A people can be oppressed, but it takes individuals to seek freedom.

It is a wonderful thing to be young and Black today. The world is in the process of redefining itself. Those of you who will make a positive difference are those of you preparing yourself for the future. Your sacrifice is worth it. The slurs you take are worth it. The racists with whom we live have nothing to do with us. We are about our Father's business. We know there are many mansions in His house. We are now looking for keys that open the doors. Don't get down on yourself. Don't let shortsighted people make you feel bad. There is something out there that only the sensibility of African-Americans can understand. "Don't let nobody turn you 'round." Know who you are; then you'll know where you are going.

CAMPUS RACISM 101

There is a bumper sticker that reads: TOO BAD IGNORANCE ISN'T PAINFUL. I like that. But ignorance is. We just seldom attribute the pain to it or even recognize it when we see it. Like the postcard on my corkboard. It shows a young man in a very hip jacket smoking a cigarette. In the background is a high school with the American flag waving. The caption says: "Too cool for school. Yet too stupid for the real world." Out of the mouth of the young man is a bubble enclosing the words "Maybe I'll start a band." There could be a postcard showing a jock in a uniform saying, "I don't need school. I'm going to the NFL or NBA." Or one showing a young man or woman studying and a group of young people saying, "So you want to be white." Or something equally demeaning. We need to quit it.

I am a professor of English at Virginia Tech. I've been here for four years, though for only two years with academic rank. I am tenured, which means I have a teaching position for life, a rarity on a predominantly white campus.

Whether from malice or ignorance, people who think I should be at a predominantly Black institution will ask, "Why are you at Tech?" Because it's here. And so are Black students. But even if Black students weren't here, it's painfully obvious that this nation and this world cannot allow white students to go through higher education without interacting with Blacks in authoritative positions. It is equally clear that predominantly Black colleges cannot accommodate the numbers of Black students who want and need an education.

Is it difficult to attend a predominantly white college? Compared with what? Being passed over for promotion because you lack credentials? Being turned down for jobs because you are not college-educated? Joining the armed forces or going to jail because you cannot find an alternative to the streets? Let's have a little perspective here. Where can you go and what can you do that frees you from interacting with the white American mentality? You're going to interact; the only question is, will you be in some control of yourself and your actions, or will you be controlled by others? I'm going to recommend self-control.

What's the difference between prison and college? They both prescribe your behavior for a given period of time. They both allow you to read books and develop your writing. They both give you time alone to think and time with your peers to talk about issues. But four years of prison doesn't give you a passport to greater opportunities. Most likely that time only gives you greater knowledge of how to get back in. Four years of college gives you an opportunity not only to lift yourself but to serve your people effectively. What's the difference when you are called nigger in college from when you are called nigger in prison? In college you can, though I admit with effort, follow procedures to have those students who called you nigger kicked out or suspended. You can bring issues to public attention without risking your life. But mostly, college is and always has been the future. We, neither less nor more than other people, need knowledge. There are discomforts attached to attending predominantly white colleges, though no more so than living in a racist world. Here are some rules to follow that may help:

Go to class. No matter how you feel. No matter how you think the professor feels about you. It's important to have a consistent presence in the classroom. If nothing else, the professor will know you care enough and are serious enough to be there.

Meet your professors. Extend your hand (give a firm handshake) and tell them your name. Ask them what you need to do to make an A. You may never make an A, but you have put them on notice that you are serious about getting good grades.

Do assignments on time. Typed or computer-generated. You have the syllabus. Follow it, and turn those papers in. If for some reason you can't complete an assignment on time, let your professor know before it is due and work out a new due date—then meet it.

Go back to see your professor. Tell him or her your name again. If an assignment received less than an A, ask why, and find out what you need to do to improve the next assignment.

Yes, your professor is busy. So are you. So are your parents who are working to pay or help with your tuition. Ask early what you need to do if you feel you are starting to get into academic trouble. Do not wait until you are failing.

Understand that there will be professors who do not like you; there may even be professors who are racist or sexist or both. You must discriminate among your professors to see who will give you the help you need. You may not simply say, "They are all against me." They aren't. They mostly don't care. Since you are the one who wants to be educated, find the people who want to help.

Don't defeat yourself. Cultivate your friends. Know your enemies. You cannot undo hundreds of years of prejudicial thinking. Think for yourself and speak up. Raise your hand in class. Say what you believe no matter how awkward you may think it sounds. You will improve in your articulation and confidence.

Participate in some campus activity. Join the newspaper staff. Run for office. Join a dorm council. Do something that involves you on campus. You are going to be there for four years, so let your presence be known, if not felt.

You will inevitably run into some white classmates who are troubling because they often say stupid things, ask stupid questions—and expect an answer. Here are some comebacks to some of the most common inquiries and comments:

Q: What's it like to grow up in a ghetto?
A: I don't know.

Q (from the teacher): Can you give us the Black perspective on Toni Morrison, Huck Finn, slavery, Martin Luther King, Jr., and others?
A: I can give you *my* perspective. (Do not take the burden of 22 million people on your shoulders. Remind everyone that you are an individual, and don't speak for the race or any other individual within it.)

Q: Why do all the Black people sit together in the dining hall?

A: Why do all the white students sit together?

Q: Why should there be an African-American studies course?

A: Because white Americans have not adequately studied the contributions of Africans and African-Americans. Both Black and white students need to know our total common history.

Q: Why are there so many scholarships for "minority" students?

A: Because they wouldn't give my great-grandparents their forty acres and the mule.

Q: How can whites understand Black history, culture, literature, and so forth?

A: The same way we understand white history, culture, literature, and so forth. That is why we're in school: to learn.

Q: Should whites take African-American studies courses?

A: Of course. We take white-studies courses, though the universities don't call them that.

Comment: When I see groups of Black people on campus, it's really intimidating.

Comeback: I understand what you mean. I'm frightened when I see white students congregating.

Comment: It's not fair. It's easier for you guys to get into college than for other people.

Comeback: If it's so easy, why aren't there more of us?

Comment: It's not our fault that America is the way it is.
Comeback: It's not our fault, either, but both of us have a responsibility to make changes.

It's really very simple. Educational progress is a national concern; education is a private one. Your job is not to educate white people; it is to obtain an education. If you take the racial world on your shoulders, you will not get the job done. Deal with yourself as an individual worthy of respect, and make everyone else deal with you the same way. College is a little like playing grown-up. Practice what you want to be. You have been telling your parents you are grown. Now is your chance to act like it.

A THEORY OF PATIENCE

Sometimes it is good to state the obvious: We cannot have a republican form of government and illiteracy. We can have, and have had, a republican form of government and preliteracy, but illiteracy indicates a willful ignorance, whether by choice of the individual or of the state. This, in either case, is unacceptable.

I believe in public education. I believe this nation made the right decision when we decided education should be open to all. Each of us here, however, knows that there was a distance between the ideal and the practice. In the South, people my age went to segregated schools even after the Brown decision; even now. Precious time was lost in our region trying to subvert a correct decision to both desegregate and to integrate the schools. Though those are two different goals, either one would have been acceptable, since good intentions could be ascribed to either. We disgracefully and hypocritically tried to sidestep the natural, logical, correct decision that we Americans will be as one. Equal protection in fact as well as theory. It would be good if all that was so much water under the bridge, but we are still living with a lingering racism that acknowledges quite frankly, "We would rather be white than right." This is unacceptable.

We have raped and neglected our urban schools all across this country. We are still looking for a way to avoid facing the errors of the past and to head ourselves toward a more homogeneous future. If we are to maintain the freedoms this nation has articulated so well, we must be about the business of fully appreciating all the various contributions of the various people who make up the body politic we call America.

It is clear to me that if there is any one crying need in our educational system, it is for the humanities to assert themselves. The disgraceful legacy of racism has made the idealism of the humanities want to go hide itself under a bush. The humanities approaches itself with a fear and trembling, hiding under pseudoscientific methods and jargon. The result is that students do not know any of the ideas that inform our body politic; they do not have any context by which to judge either words or actions. Our young people, and we see it every day in the violence in our schools and neighborhoods, have no context by which to set their standards of personal behavior. They imitate what they see . . . violence, and a "might makes right" philosophy . . . imitating the impotence and ignorance around them. Only the humanities are qualified to carry us through this more difficult period of adjustment; only the humanities are capable of gentling the spirit of human beings, allowing a more serene patience to prevail.

I am only a poet and therefore have no training in educational theories. I know we like to blame television for the lack of reading skills and the lack of interest in books. Yet the stupid, insulting, dumb books that we give to students will turn them against reading on their own. Students will read if there is a good story; if there is a hero to admire and a problem to overcome. Whether or not the protagonist wins, the journey through the tears is worthwhile. We have neutered books, censored teachers who have tried to present good, interesting books, quarreled in higher education about which books students should be familiar with, and yet we continue to expect our students to be readers? I think not. In the universities we have seen white men declare time and time again that they cannot teach women, they cannot teach Blacks, they cannot teach Native Americans, because they do not have any "experience" in this area. Yet we who are Black and women and not white males are expected to teach literature written by them because it is "universal"? I think not. It is called education because it is learned. You do not have to have had an experience in order to sympathize or empathize with the subject. That is why books are written: so that we do not have to do the same things. We learn from experience, true; but we also learn from empathy. The colleges and universities want to *talk* about multicultural, but they do not want to *be* multicultural. I am not one who likes the term "role model," yet I believe that the greatest good higher education can do for primary and secondary education is to be a model of a multicultural society. As long as higher education remains all white, the message we send is in our actions, not in our words. As long as higher education considers itself "higher," with all of the privileges but none of the attendant responsibilities, then hypocrisy is the lesson our students learn. We in the universities and colleges must close the gap between what we say and what we do. Only then can we justify the citizenry spending time and money on us.

In elementary and secondary education, the most obvious need is for students to have their families involved in their education. The schools must be open to parents and, if I may say so, grandparents. If I could persuade my university to lend me out, I would love to start a pilot study on twenty-four-hour schools. I would have students in one part of the building in the day and their grandparents in another. I know that older people have stories to tell, and I know that we can more easily teach a storyteller to write than to read. The desire to put the story on paper can lead a generation that has shunned books into an acceptance of the need for help. A Black presence can also help overcome the older generation's fears of the different and the unknown. I would also want an evening program for the parents. The family workshops don't have to be scheduled every day, but they should be weekly. The parents should be in some sort of workshop where they interact with different people. I mention the need for writers' workshops because everybody has at least one story: his/her own. A great stumbling block to learning is the attitude of the family/community. We need to open the doors to our schools to everyone. We invite them to our basketball, football, soccer games. We want parents to come to plays and support other activities. Why not pay our teachers enough, and hire enough teachers to service the needs of the communities?

I am, of course, not being practical here. There are probably money considerations, and money is not to be ignored. Yet, if we do not ask, we will never know. Americans have risen to each and every occasion. I think our teachers will reach down and try once again. It is also fair to point out that as long as we pay coaches and administrators disproportionately to teachers, as long as we "reward" teachers by taking them out of the classroom and kicking them into administration, we are sending a message that teaching is not so very important after all. Money, by the way, would help. It would also help if principals and school boards weren't so quick to CYA (Cover Your Ass) when parents and others raise questions. Education, in other words, has to be more than just a job . . . it is a great responsibility . . . and the future is at stake.

The nation has been excited to reform colleges and universities, to make better college graduates and therefore make America more competitive, but if trickle-down doesn't work in economics, it doesn't work in education either. There is no effective way to reform colleges other than to reform and improve secondary education. Our colleges are servants of secondary education, not masters; we need to put the shoe on the correct foot. Our energy and money must first go to public schools, from preschool to high school graduation, encouraging the student, teacher, and community to be better citizens, more informed citizens, more productive citizens.

We must reclaim the humanities to remind us that patience is a human virtue; we must integrate racially to show ourselves fear cannot always determine human possibilities. We have a world to conquer . . . one person at a time . . . starting with ourselves.

IV

"BUT COMMON THINGS SURPRISE US"

—GWENDOLYN BROOKS

COFFEE SIGNS

My grandparents lived on Mulvaney Street in Knoxville. For the longest time I sang, "Here we go 'round the mulvaney bush," being quite sure at that young age that others were mispronouncing. Is it that things seem so much better with age or from a distance? I'm sure I was bored many an evening as we three sat on the front porch watching the JFG COFFEE sign flick on and off . . . on and off. Yet it is a peaceful memory. I loved the sound of the train whistle. It always seemed to bring rain. Logic says the whistle blew at other times, and in any rational system I would know that it was only on rainy days that I was in the house to hear it. Yet even now a train whistle brings the smell of rain to me, the dark clouds, flashes of lightning, and the warmth of sitting in the living room listening to Grandpapa tell stories until the storm had passed. Nothing is learned until the spirit incorporates it; nothing has passed until it is forgotten. Knoxville and I may change, should change, but there will always be, for me, that porch facing the tennis courts of Cal Johnson Park and, at a forty-five-degree angle, the lights of JFG COFFEE flicking on and off . . . on and off . . . and the two people with whom I sat.

A LETTER FROM NIKKI

Dear Pearl,

I have wrestled with your letter most of the summer. As much as I believe all writers are navel contemplators and actually think on some days that we may, in fact, be egomaniacs, I find I have nothing new or interesting to say about myself autobiographically. I've looked at my childhood, the way I write, anything that I think can be interesting, and I am not finding anything. Not that I don't think I am interesting—just not all that interesting. And then I had the additional problem of trying to decide if I am inside or outside. I wander but I carry my world with me, so I couldn't decide if I am a dreamer or a wanderer. I think all writers are dreamers, because why else would we do this, yet if I could I'd take the space shuttle. My problem by now is becoming evident to you.

Plus my child reached his majority. I am about to agree with the folks who say that's a difficult time for parents. I used to think, oh well, the kid will be gone, but you really do miss the little buggers. I went out Saturday and bought myself a candy-apple-red-MR2, which I do recognize to be arrested adolescence, but somehow youth cannot be recaptured. Though in all fairness to the car, an MR2 comes close.

So that's a long way of saying I'm having one of my infrequent, though nonetheless serious, periods of personality crisis. A name that I carried for eighteen years has been, not deleted, because I will always be his mother, but sort of not needed. I think I must be having some insight into how people feel who are forced to retire. Or even how people who are glad to retire feel. You like to think you've done a good job and all, but then you are saying, "Well, shit, what am I going to do with myself?"

Having sworn I would not give up my bell bottoms, I turned around about the end of August (just before he turned eighteen) and threw out all my pants. I think I am trying to be reborn in a secular sense. Anyway, you want to look your age (because I like my age), but there is still a need to make some change that says to yourself you'll be all right.

At any rate and in conclusion, as they say, I didn't do your essay because I can't quite figure out who I am right now other than a forty-four-year-old woman adjusting to a totally new and largely unplanned obsolescence that I am proud of but regret. So if you do autobiographical stuff after I figure out where I'm going, I'll be able to tell you where I've been.

Nikki

MEMORIES ARE SELECTIVE

Our first home in Cincinnati was at Glenview School, where my parents were headmaster and wife. I say "wife" because she, like the first lady, came with the territory and, while not being paid, was expected to uphold all the good and truthful standards of doing things correctly while, also on the side, providing love and inspiration to the head-master and boys. I don't actually remember Glenview School. I've heard family stories about being there, though there is one memory that I think I own: I fell down the second-floor stairs, tumbling, tumbling like a slinky. Mommy thought I had perhaps broken my neck or some-thing serious; I was worried about my doll, which, thank goodness, was rubber.

We moved at some point to Woodlawn, where I have memories of being bathed in the kitchen, a wonderful thing that has spoiled me to this day and made me yearn for a bathroom that is a room and not a closet. We had an outhouse that was wonderful because you could go out there and no one knocked on the door telling you it was bedtime or that they had to comb their hair or something. Recently I mentioned that when I hit one of the three state lotteries that I periodically play I would build a round house with an outhouse because I thought they were so neat. Someone asked me, "What did you do in the winter? Wasn't it cold?" I'm sure I urinated in the winter, as it is illogical to think I could get through a winter without doing so, yet I have no memory of plodding through the snow and cold. But I learned something from that question: Memories are selective. If people tell us good things, we remember the good; when they tell us bad things, we remember that. Freud is not right: we don't, I feel, remember childhood so much as we remember what we are told about it.

Our next home was in Wyoming, Ohio, a suburb of Cincinnati, at 1038 Burns Avenue. I remember my kindergarten teacher, Mrs. Hicks, and my first-grade teacher, Miss Scott. She was probably Mrs. Scott, but that isn't how I perceived her. My sister and I went to Oak Avenue School, which later became a YMCA and, later still, a police station, if memory serves me correctly. Mother says I was not happy to attend kindergarten, preferring to stay at home with her. She is probably right, since, to this day, I prefer to stay at home with Mother rather than venture forth into a cold and indifferent world. By my fourth-grade year we had moved to Lincoln Heights, where we still have a home. My sister Gary attended South Woodlawn, and I went with Mother to her first job at St. Simon's School.

South Woodlawn only went to the eighth grade; after that children in Lincoln Heights had our choice of high schools. You could take a test and, passing, go to Walnut

Hills. A lot of our Lincoln Heighters went to Taft and Withrow. Gary chose Wyoming.

I don't think I had a conception of "integrating" at that point, but Gary was among the first Black students to attend Wyoming High. I know Beverly Waugh attended, as did Yvonne Rogers. I think Jimmy Morris had gone some time before they did. I do remember thinking when I saw Wyoming High that it was a wonderful building. Once when Oak Avenue did not have heat we youngsters all had to go to Wyoming High for classes for a couple of days. Although I don't have any memories of specific events, I do recall that we did not know our counterparts, and they did not know us. At recess we did not play together. I know I was glad to get back to my own school. The Wyoming High that I remember is now the Wyoming Middle School on Wyoming Avenue. Gary had lunch at school, and that was exciting to me. They made a thing called "hamburger shortcake" every Friday, and the way Gary described it, it was heaven. There is a taste in my mouth that can only be memory of a succulent hamburger, covered with gravy served on a shortcake bun. It was just too sophisticated for words. I could hardly wait for Gary to come home from school to ask: "Did they serve it again?" And she would describe it once more. I've never attempted to make hamburger shortcake, since I know the reality would, of necessity, fall grievously short.

She made a friend, Jeannie Evans, who shopped at Jenny's. Mommy, never wanting us to lack what others had, opened a charge account at Jenny's that we still use. And Gary was hit in the face with a basketball in gym. There was no question but that it was racist. The girl who did it did it deliberately because Gary was Black. I remember her face was red in a round circle and Gus, our father, made one of his many trips to see Bradbury, the superintendent of schools. Everyone was shocked and saddened by the event. Apologies were made all around. But what I recall is that someone hit my sister for no reason. Her teacher in civics, a still-needed course that is no longer taught, discussed the Emmett Till case with his class. "Till got what he deserved," he declared. Gary and Beverly walked out, and Gus made another trip to see Bradbury. Apologies all around. Shock and sadness that this could happen. I was sent to Knoxville, Tennessee, to live with my grandmother when the Princeton school district was integrating. Our family had already given a soldier to the war to make white Americans better people.

I am an unreconstructed Trekkie. Man (read humans) was meant to fly. Sometimes we get confused and think flight is a physical thing: something to do with engines or wings made of wax. Everybody told Icarus that if he used those wings when he got near the sun they would melt. I don't really know if Icarus simply did not believe them or if he thought his wings could withstand the heat, but he took off with the instruments available . . . and he failed. Or did he? Didn't he, in reality, simply fall back to earth? And can it be a failure when our goal is to reach higher? I think not. Had Columbus slipped off the ocean into the darkness we probably would not know him now, but he would have been just as successful as if he had sailed right up to India. There are some things we do simply because the doing is a success. We try to treat people fairly; we try to live our lives with dignity; we try, in our hearts and minds, to "go boldly where no man has gone." And isn't that the ultimate contribution we make to the human experiment? We young writers raise the questions of our time. We seek to expose the unacceptable and to celebrate the wonderful. We seek to "kiss the sky," because earth is our home, not our destiny. Our destiny is a better universe where we can live together in peace and understanding.

NOVEMBER 22

November was clear though seasonably cool in 1963. I remember the sun was shining. Mother had purchased a white, convertible Nova that she let me drive. It was too cool to have the top down, but any University of Cincinnati student with a convertible would at least sport the windows, which I did. Morning classes went as morning classes do. Students half asleep; professors muttering to themselves that there must be a better way to earn a living. My classes finished around noon. I would leave campus, then go to my job at Walgreen's. Walgreen's Drugstore was a perfect job for me because it kept my mind focused on school. No one wanted to grow up to be a floor girl for a drugstore. As I was crossing the campus to the car, someone said, "Kennedy has been shot." A group of students gathered and the person, I don't remember whether male or female, said Kennedy and Connally were shot in Texas. I hurried on to my car, thinking, "If one of them has to die, I hope it's Connally."

I immediately turned the radio on. The early reports were muddled. Johnson was all right. No other news. By the time I got to Walgreen's, about a ten-minute drive, they were announcing Kennedy's death. We on the floor wore white smocks. I put my smock on and walked rather aimlessly around. I was waiting for Richard, our manager, to close the store. I could see no sense in remaining open. After an hour or so, Richard announced that we would remain open. Because I was junior on the floor, I had already worked the Fourth of July and Labor Day. I had worked Halloween, and on another job I had worked both Thanksgiving and Christmas. It wasn't work. I never minded working.

I don't remember having any thoughts that history was changing or that the country had taken an irrevocable step backward. I just couldn't see the sense in my trying to locate Sal Hepatica for some customer or sell perfume. I went downstairs, put my smock back in my locker, and punched out. Richard saw me as I came back upstairs. He had a rule against employees parking in front of the store, which I had a habit of doing. "You are supposed to be at work," he said. I said I'd be back later. It wasn't a challenge; I didn't care to discuss it. It just didn't make sense, on November 22, 1963, to stay at work.

VIRGINIA: MY VIEW

I like rain. That has to be one of the main reasons I live in the southwestern part of Virginia. If I didn't like rain I'd have to move to Arizona or New Mexico or even back to Ohio because it rains all the time here. Well, not all the time . . . just more than not. I found out—not that it was a secret—the year after I moved from Cincinnati to Blacksburg that Virginia Tech was located in Blacksburg because it rains here more than in any other part of the state. Of course, when you're being recruited, they sort of forget to mention that. No one says, "Come to Blacksburg and experience our rain."

Actually, other than "Where do you live?" I only know one question that throws me off: Why did you do something? Where do you live? throws me off because I have room space from New York to Cincinnati to San Francisco. I have, in fact, found this a pleasant way to live. I never have to carry luggage; I only have to remember where I left something. My wardrobe is quite slight and duplicated, so that has not proved to be a problem through the years. Why I live like a nomad is more difficult. Well, not actually more difficult, because the answer is: It is convenient. You can hardly run a career, rear a child, raise a couple of dogs, and have any sanity if you throw in window washing, stopped toilets, gutters that need cleaning in fall, furnaces that need filters changed . . . the rather normal things that go with a house. I thought I'd try a noble experience of letting my son know that home is where we are . . . not a building nor a place . . . not things but a feeling. I had to work because I have never been able to get six numbers together for any lottery. If he and Wendy, our cairn terrier, went to work with me, then I could have my family. All the advantages of home and few of the disadvantages.

After we acquired Bruno, Tom's dog, things began to change. Plus Tom needed to go to school, so we became apartment dwellers, then condo dwellers, then we did the really intelligent thing and moved back to Cincinnati to live with my mother and father after Gus, my father, had a stroke. People, in their kindness, want to say what a wonderful thing I did to give up my home and independence to go back to my parents' home, but the wonderful thing for me was that two people I have known and loved needed me and I needed them. Being a grown-up in my parents' home was no problem. They told me what to do and I did it. Simple. Gus was sick; Tom was a child. My mother and I traded off, and the household ran very smoothly. Unfortunately, though not unexpectedly, my father died and my son grew up. Wendy, my dog, succumbed to cancer. That just left the two of us and Bruno. I was worried, not without reason, that Mommy and I would become two little old ladies in Ohio. I would con-

tinue to work; she would retire. We would hold our an-
nual chitterling dinner and see friends, but we wouldn't be
contributing to the world. It takes very little for me to
close down. My profession is a close-down profession. If I
didn't make myself go out and see people, I stood a good
chance of becoming what a lot of writers are: insular and
indifferent to the real world.

Then one late fall or early winter morning came a letter
from Virginia Fowler, associated head of English at Vir-
ginia Tech, inviting me to apply for Visiting Common-
wealth Professor. Mommy had never even stepped foot in
Virginia. We knew the Blacksburg area because we are
from Knoxville, which is four hours due west at sixty-five
miles per hour, but she had never crossed that state line
and wasn't that excited to do so until Doug Wilder be-
came governor. Mom and Bruno went to San Francisco.
Tom would soon be graduating from high school and, as
children are wont to do, probably going on with his life.
I'm not a great believer in the empty-nest syndrome, but
Mom and I were facing it. I flew over to visit Tech and, I
suppose, be looked over. Thinking Virginia was in the
South, I carried nice summer clothes. First mistake. South-
western Virginia gets cold and snow and rain. But Tech is
impossible to dislike. Tech has the greatest youngsters in
Virginia, a good faculty, a dean who looks like he would
just as soon roll up his sleeves and bake a loaf of cinnamon
bread. I actually wasn't busy, so I came to Tech.

Being a visiting professor is not like having a real job.
I was teaching a literature course and a writing course. I've
long known the most important people in any organiza-
tion are the secretaries, but I had no idea that ours could
cook, too. Leota and I exchanged recipes; Tammy and I
argued over who made the best beans. I've got to say that

for a white girl she's not half bad. Our janitorial staff was friendly. Maybe I put too much stock in support services, but when the support services are good, the institution will follow. I've never known an institution with indifferent grounds keepers that meant anyone well. It's easy for the top to be friendly—they are well paid and well benefited for it; the others speak from the heart. I met Tech's interim provost, John Perry, and one just simply does not say no to John. There are three gentlemen at Tech: Perry; Burke Johnston, who is retired; and Hil Campbell, who ultimately stepped down as English Department head. I've heard about the Texas gentleman and the Virginia gentleman and it's not that you can't say no to them; you simply don't want to. You talk with them a while and you feel smart and witty and charming and just ever so needed. I fell in love.

There is always a difference between courtship and marriage. I've gotten to know Tech a lot better and see our needs a lot clearer. If Tech is to reach its full potential as a great institution, we need to accept our regional challenge. We need to reach into Giles County, which has some wonderful elementary school children who should, right now, be involved with Tech; we need a Black presence in Vinton, which seems to need, to paraphrase T. S. Eliot, another turning of another stair; we need to understand that we do not compete with UVA but with Charlotte. People should be looking to Tech for more than football. A real theater would help; a real concert series would help; more national speakers would help; a jazz series; a country and western series; a recognition that we face biracial problems, not multicultural. We get along fine with international folk; it's the homegrown normal Black Americans who cause us to stumble or over whom we constantly seem to trip. Our white youngsters cannot be allowed to reach around the Black to the yellow and the brown. But these are details. Roanoke calls itself the "Star City," and it's poised to be so. Roanoke offers some of the South's greatest craftspeople; we have a symphony and ballet; we have Artemis for writers and performers. All the elements are in place for southwest Virginia. And we have those gorgeous mountains.

Sociologists ponder why people would stay in these mountains with the bad, rocky soil, with the winter snow and the spring floods. I don't. They are majestic. The mountains and the people make this area one of the hidden gems of eastern America. Just to awake to the fog lifting from the valley; to see the sun, on I-81 as you roll into Roanoke from Blacksburg, break the clouds. . . . No, I don't wonder at all why people chose to live here. Maple Anderson, a friend, colleague, and Democratic party stalwart, once ran for an office in the party. She and her husband had just moved to Virginia from Maine. Her right to represent Virginia was questioned by her opponent. She said: "All Black Americans come from Virginia. We all *landed* here. Some of us just went somewhere else for a while." I think she's right. I live here because it's home. And hey, even the predictability of the rain is less unnerving once you get properly outfitted.

SISTERS, TOO

Almost every Friday four of us get together to play bid whist. Three of us are mothers; all of us are aunts. One of us has sons and daughters; two of us have an "only," one daughter and one son. Three of us have nephews and nieces; one of us has only a nephew.

Maple and I were behind, nothing that a couple of no-trumps wouldn't eventually clear up, but Maple was distracted. She was leaving the next morning for Oklahoma City to pin her niece. I shouldn't say "distracted," because the proper word is *excited*. Her family tradition of Delta Sigma Theta would go on. I have only a son and a nephew. It hit me. I had not really considered it before. But I, by having no daughters or nieces, have no one to pass a tradition on to. No one who would love the table-cloths my grandmother had passed down nor the silver she had purchased one place setting at a time. No one to admire the crystal vase we had purchased together and into which we put the prize roses Grandmother had grown. My mother had two daughters, each of whom took different aspects of her personality. She could see herself in us, even, or perhaps especially, now that we were well into our middle age. We kept her things and had an affection for them. The world is so boy-prone that, having had only a boy, women rarely think, To whom will I pass my sorority pin? Who will drink from the glasses my grandmother saved from her mother's possessions? Who will iron and patch the old tablecloths? Who will air the quilts? I guess I have always understood man's love of his sons, but there is an equal, and compelling, reason women love our daughters.

I have always wanted to be a good daughter. I have wanted to make my mother and grandmother proud of me. I like to think I am a good mother; at least I know I did my best.

There is always the history of Phillis Wheatley writing the first poems of note published in Colonial America; there is the glorious history of Harriet Tubman leading slaves to freedom. There is the unsurpassed courage of Mary Church Terrell crusading with her pen for the abolition of lynching; of Rosa Parks having the vision of sitting down to stand up for what is right. Emmett Till's mother opened the casket to say to the world, "Look what they did to my son." Shirley Chisholm running for president. There is also the quiet courage of mothers counseling patience in the face of brutality; offering hope in the face of despair. The women who taught the little girls how to iron the sheets and shirts; how to darn a pair of socks; how to pretend, when they became mothers, that they didn't need a new coat or want a new dress so that their children could have a bit more.

It is an honorable calling: womanhood. And a wonderful thing when we not only take up the task of gentling the spirit but passing our faith along.

I offered Maple the pin my mother was pinned with. My father, for their first wedding anniversary, had replaced the original pin with a Delta Sigma Theta with pearls in the beloved Sigma. He could not afford that. But he must have understood that one day she would have daughters who would need the pin more than he needed whatever the money spent would have bought.

Mommy was tapped for one sorority; others have made different choices. What we do know and applaud is the community of women, whether Greek or not, who come together to say to the daughters—now you are my sister, too.

Three of us write. One is a poet; two are scholar-critics. One of us is a widow. Every Friday, almost, we come together, answering the ancient call Gloria Naylor so beautifully expressed: "Sister, you still here?"

MY ROAD TO VIRGINIA

There always seems to be a Virginia connection. I didn't come to Virginia because I thought Doug Wilder would be elected governor, though I'm delighted that he was; and I'm not staying in Virginia because he'll probably go on to be at least vice president, though I'm delighted that he most likely, if this is a fair world, will be. My very own Ohio majority leader, Bill Mallory, is just as good a candidate, though not as visible. It's funny that race is less a factor in the former home of the Confederacy than in a free state. But . . . hey . . . times change or not, according to ebbs and flows I will never fathom. I came to Virginia because I was offered a job.

In a way I hate to look at the previous sentence. Someone is bound to say, "But you could get a job anywhere." I like to think that's true, too, but I can't. I'm a writer who does, I believe, know something about writing. I may even know something about thinking. I certainly know something about giving, but I don't know, and I'm proud to confess I have no interest in, what someone who never in this life had to face a public, thinks about what someone else, who did, wrote. Was that an awkward sentence? I'm not an academic who is contemptuous of the people and the judgment of the people. I don't believe my "higher calling" in life allows me to be an insecure professor who gets her rocks off by not teaching students. I do believe in service. I know, I know . . . someone is saying, "Well, what are you doing at a research institution?" I like to think, on a good day, that I'm helping others to recognize that higher education's gravy train not only is over but should be.

Teaching is an honorable profession. I, in fact, come from a long line of teachers. My grandfather taught Latin in Knoxville, Tennessee, public schools; my grandmother taught in Albany, Georgia, Normal School. Both my mother and father taught, third grade and eighth grade respectively, until their growing family forced them to look for higher-paying jobs. My aunts, Agnes and Ann, taught in public schools and college; my uncle, Clinton Marsh, was president of Knoxville College. There is no one outside my immediate family I hold in higher esteem than Alfredda Delaney, who taught English in my high school, Austin. Madame Emma Stokes tried to get me to learn French. Miss Delaney recently passed on, but Madame Stokes is still with us, and I still consider her a friend. Perhaps these are not real credentials, but I bring a high expectation to the profession. Our first job is to teach.

When I graduated from college in 1964, the only true credential I had for a job was that I was pretty good at picketing. As many have since learned, being a sixties person does not serve as a qualifier. It does mean, most times though, that you are a believer. I could add that being a history major also was not what would be considered an asset. Of course, business has since discovered that it is far better off with a good history or English major than a business or computer person, but that discovery missed my bloom. I was not opposed to being a writer, but despite the changes coming, color-wise, in America, there were and are very few Blacks in the newsrooms, magazines, or free-lance market; publishers were not interested in more than one Black writer at a time. Opportunity was limited. I applied to graduate school.

My dream, at that time, was to win a Woodrow Wilson Scholarship and attend the University of Chicago, where I would make startling and profound discoveries in history. I would follow in the footsteps of John Hope Franklin, my fellow Fisk alumnus, making important connections between behavior and history, perhaps even testifying before Congress as to the effects, historically and currently, of racism on both victim and victimizer. I would settle down in some small college town, read and write books, teach (and be a very demanding teacher) young people a new way of looking at the world. I had an Afro, however, and Mr. Currier, the head of history, didn't think I had the right attitude to succeed in graduate school. He was probably right. Fortunately for me, Blanche Cowan, the dean of women, was a Penn graduate in social work. She thought my crusading should be put to use, and off I went to Philadelphia.

I never did make it through grad school. My year at Penn was great because social work is a wonderful background for any humanities person. Dr. Louise Shoemaker thought I was more suited to writing and suggested I should give myself a chance in that field. I'm sure she could have put it more bluntly, but she was a friend. And why did I have a difficult time in the M.S.W. program? I'm not institution-prone. Most times, in any dispute between an institution and a person, I take the side of a person. The human has to be found seriously wanting for my vote to sway the other way. Obviously, you aren't going to go far in social work if you are unwilling to keep records on clients. I kept records. Some of my best young writing was done while I was in social work school with my agency placement records. I simply didn't want to put name and judgments in the records. They read like wonderful short stories—hardly what my social work professors were after. Columbia University . . . here I come.

I still feel that Columbia owes me an M.F.A. Our job, once we were accepted into the program, was, over a two-year period, to produce a book. We were allowed to take other courses, but they were not required. We were to meet, read our work, receive criticism, correct our work, and come back the next week to do it again. Within the first year I had finished my first book. Fearing, as I always have, rejection, I started a publishing company and produced my first book, *Black Feeling/Black Talk*. Was it a great book? I don't think so, but it was honest, clear, and perhaps a bit bold. My writing professor at Columbia invited me to his home, where he gently explained that I would not go far with my poetry. I should temper it and find my way in academia. Thanks, Richard. I refused that advice, dropped out of school, and decided to go for broke. Or probably, more honestly, admitted I was broke, had been born broke, and would die broke, and decided not to worry about it ever again.

Since I was now the head of a publishing firm, I needed to make a go of it. I had borrowed money from family and friends, which is, I think, different from borrowing from banks and institutions. The books sold. I did have the sense to keep a competitive price on them. I also took a page from Langston Hughes, who had died two years before I got to New York, and took my books to the people. Rutgers University was opening a new campus, Livingston, and I was recommended by Toni Cade to teach. I accepted. This was a time of great activism, so I think we were expected more to contain than teach students. I learned a lot about the failure of high schools in New Jersey and made a lifelong friend of one student, Debbie Russell. Deb, by the way, traveled all over the world with me, moved to Cincinnati when I moved back, married a wonderful man, has three robust children, and went back to college, after her Rutgers graduation, to polish her skills. Rutgers failed Debbie, but she had the strength and support to push forward. It failed many other Black students, also.

Like most New York writers, I've taught a course at the New School for Social Research. I taught in the SEEK program on Long Island. But I didn't really get back into a real classroom until I was a visiting professor at Ohio State. That was a great experience; the students were excellent. Not that other students weren't, but these students made the classroom a jazz band. Everybody already knew the music; we could play variations. English didn't have any regular, tenured Black faculty, and I was not interested in trying to become one, but it did put something on my mind. The College of Mount St. Joseph, headed by one of the great educators of our time, Sister Jean Patrice Harrington, took a courageous stand on free speech. I would not rest until I called Sr. Jean, and having no money to donate, offered my time. I taught creative writing for the Mount for two years and loved every minute of it. Most of my students were nontraditional, as they say; older would be the other word. Sr. Jean persuaded businesses to contribute to the Mount and have that contribution work toward tuition for an employee. It was a great program that worked well for the Mount, business, and the employees. The Mount had no Black full-time faculty either, and has now lost Linda Dixon, in academic planning, to Miami of Ohio. One does have to wonder. Between 12 and 14 percent of all Americans are Black. We couldn't all be that busy.

Virginia Tech called at a time in my life when I was no longer committed. My son was graduating from high school and going on, as it turned out, to two years in the army. My mother and I had lived together since the illness of my father. I thought it would do us both good to make a change of scene. Mommy held no affection for Virginia and she declined to join me in Blacksburg. I decided to come; and having come, to stay. By now there were certain things I had learned. Come as "full" professor or come "tenured." I came "full"; we would have to see if we liked each other enough to accept tenure. My colleagues were wonderful my first year. Everybody was so happy I was there. Then my second year it dawned on some people: If I stayed I would be the first woman in the English Department who would be tenured full. As a Commonwealth Visiting Professor, I was accepted; as a tenured full with a mind of my own, I was not. I was surprised to discover myself engaged in a struggle to remain at Tech.

Why did I agree to fight against those who so glibly dismissed my achievements—to whom my sixteen books, my honors and awards, my twenty years in public life, simply didn't count? I decided to stay and fight because I want the future to be determined by the best of Virginia

Tech, a microcosm of higher education, and not by its worst. Virginia Fowler, associate head of English, led the charge. John Perry, provost, and ultimately when he took office, James McComas, president, wanted me to stay. I also know that it's important that somebody stay. For sure you can jump around to other institutions and improve, greatly I might add, your paycheck. But at some point the institution and the people who serve it must recognize that their failure to bring Black professors on board is a faculty failure to vote tenure. All Black people do not have the record of support that I had, but surely most, if not all, are as qualified as their white counterparts. Had I had the meager credentials that some of my tenured colleagues have, I would have been turned down. But ... hey ... it is not new to me that I have to be better than anyone in the club in order to be admitted.

Why is it important to get Blacks into colleges and universities? Because the biggest stumbling block to progress in America is still racism. Because we have to find a way to comfort young white people about the fact that, though they will never stride atop that wonderful white horse and rule the world again, they can make valid contributions to our planet. The world is not, and has never been, white. Less so today than previously. Privilege is anathema to democracy. And the professoriate is a very privileged group. I remember all too well, during the days of segregation, not being allowed in amusement parks, theaters, and restaurants. I thought they must be wonderful things. I was never fooled by the drinking fountains, dressing rooms in department stores, waiting rooms in bus and train stations; I knew those to be nothing more than a way of inconveniencing patrons of color. But schools. They seemed special, too. We would see the white kids on their clean, undented, new bus going to and from school, to parks, museums, the zoo. Always, it seemed to me, screaming from the windows, laughing loud, throwing things; behavior that would not for one moment be tolerated in us. I remember when East High got a computer and new science lab. Our physics teacher at Austin, though very good, doubled as basketball coach. Something was wrong.

The sixties have come and gone. The United States is no longer the preeminent power in the world; we're not even nice people. White boys and girls may have always been dumb, and without the racial component they might now not have an incentive to try to excel, or maybe they were cocooned and were having the bottom described by Black people. Those white boys and girls who were not successful went on to join the Klan or the skinheads or whatever Nazi organization is available to those who are free and white and still losers. I don't know. I do know that those who come to college need to be taught that there is a larger world into which they not only can but must fit. I do know that we who are adult must adjust systems to include those who have been artificially excluded. I do well understand that while I am tenured and full it is an unjust system that awards us for avoiding the very thing we are being paid to do: teach. What do I want? An end to the tenure system. Period. An end to research on campus. If business wants to hire a professor, let it hire him or her, but mostly him, and give him the salary and benefits it gives any other employee. An end to the professionalization of sport on campus. Let the NFL and the NBA create their own training camps. Stop the whoring for television dollars and get to—it certainly is not *back* to—the idea of coaching as teaching. Treat coaches as we do any member of the professoriate. Stop the absolute nonsense of creating a migrant class of workers called the "adjunct." Higher education has increasingly come to depend on "temporary" underpaid faculty to do much of the teaching of our children, yet they can stay full-time in an institution only a brief time because of the fear that they might have a claim, after seven years, on de facto tenure. The professoriate should be ashamed of itself that it allows this system to exist. These "temporary" faculty would have more job security for a job well done if they worked in a lettuce field. Stop the graveyards called "associate heads," "assistant deans," "assistant provosts." These have become the female position on campuses; they are dead ends. Recognize, despite everything I've said, that there can be no reform without faculty. Give faculty a reason to teach again. Reward, don't punish, faculty who spend time with students. Stop encouraging the production of dumb books on dumb subjects that no one reads and that drain library resources just so some professor can say, "I wrote a book. See? It's in the library." Bring all student services, from concerts to the commissary, under faculty responsibility. In other words, give the university back to the teachers . . . and let them teach.

How will this lessen racism among faculty? We will run up against something called competence. People will have to admit what they know and don't know. Intelligent people normally seek help when they are not punished for it. I need to believe that the world can be fair. I know it will not be as long as there is a social and financial incentive to be small-minded and vindictive. I need to believe my colleagues across this country will once again take as much pride in the students they have helped as they do now in the lines of dubious publication they have produced. If

Virginia, the home of Thomas Jefferson, George Washington, Patrick Henry, Nat Turner—men who, though flawed, struck a blow for freedom—cannot accept this challenge, we are hard pressed to say where the leadership will come from. The nation looks to California for trends; it turns to Virginia for reason.

Long ago, not all that far from my home, Thomas Jefferson and others sat to chart a course for humans that would incorporate change as a constant. Virginia has stood up to the political challenge; she will accept the educational one as well. I live here because I have a job at Virginia Tech. I wouldn't want to be anyplace else.

"AT THIS LOPSIDED CRYSTAL SWEET MOMENT"

—CAROLYN M. RODGERS

ARCHITECTURE

There are some things that you love simply because you ought to: the Sistine Chapel; old English country homes; everything in the Louvre; the crown jewels; valuable things like that, which, while lovely and representing great achievement, are still quite removed from our everyday experience. There are other things you love because of the joy and comfort they bring: gospel music; the quilt your grandmother made; warm blackberry cobbler; things of incomparable worth that only the heart can judge. Since we all die, there is even a need to love every cemetery in New Orleans, and none can deny the majesty of the pyramids. Those of us who are education lovers bow to Thomas Jefferson's vision at Monticello, lamenting the loss of the great libraries of Timbuktu and Alexandria. One stands, in fact, in awe of the Constitution of the United States, though it is an idea and not quite a reality. No one can deny the power of Jesus, whether we subscribe to the various little people who have capitalized on Him or not. Ideas are structured and remain much stronger than most buildings. I love the idea of "Lucy" (the prehistoric skeleton unearthed by Donald Johannson in Ethiopia). Were I God, starting an ecosystem, I, too, would choose to put a Black woman at the center of my world with the surety that she would get things off to a proper start. The basis of all human knowledge, and therefore human action, is belief.

Albert Einstein had first to believe he could postulate a theory of E by putting it into a relationship with *mc* squared; Columbus had first to believe the world was actually round before he could decide to sail west to reach east; Pasteur had to believe those molds could do *something* before penicillin could be put to use to save human lives from disease. Rumpelstiltskin, for that matter, had to believe he could forever hide his name from the miller's daughter, though he lost his bet. And you and I have to believe we can alleviate human suffering caused by accidents of birth and circumstances by applying our skills to make this life an easier passage.

Sam Mockbee used his skills as an architect to build a better dwelling for some families in Mississippi. Who wouldn't want to live in these houses? They were actually designed by humans for humans. We know, from basic studies of our own domestic pets and animals, how important environment is to life. Polar bears don't function well in rain-forest environments; whales, though mammals, cannot function out of water; human beings do not do well in hovels or shacks, or on the streets of our major cities. Snails, we recognize, carry their houses with them, as do turtles. Humans house a soul in an imperfect body; the body needs a majestic dwelling to encourage the soul to expand. We do know that nature hates a vacuum; gases will expand to fill all unoccupied space; the heart will shrink to the space available. The lawyers and lawmakers will, of course, quibble over the meaning of "majestic," but poets have no such problem. We know we mean that which is adequate to the job at hand, and beautifully, lovingly pre-scribed for that purpose. Our urban and rural poor need Sam Mockbee; Mockbee deserves to be needed.

The job of the architect becomes more difficult in this secular age. Where once he had a god to extol, he now has humans like himself; where once he had "he," he now has "she" and "they." His task is no different from that facing any other profession based on belief: medicine, teaching, poetry, among many, many others. Are we able to believe that other human beings deserve our best? That, I believe, is the central question. I believe we, like heat or cream, can and will rise to the challenge.

BLACK AMERICAN LITERATURE:
AN INTRODUCTION

A few years ago, *Voyager 2* crossed our galaxy heading toward the Dog Star. We don't know a lot about the light that earth sees, but we know the brightest star in the galaxy is beyond the influence of the yellow sun. Galileo would be proud. I'm a Trekkie. I like the concepts of both space and the future. I'm not big on the idea of aliens who always seem to want to destroy earth and earthlings. It's almost laughable that the most destructive force in the known universe, humankind, always fears something is out there trying to get us. Freud said something about projection . . . and though I would hardly consider myself a Freudian, I think he had a point.

It's not really a question of whether or not E.T. is Black; his story is the story of sojourning. It doesn't even matter whether he came to earth to explore or was brought to earth for less honorable pursuits. He found himself left behind with neither kith nor kin to turn to. He depended, in the words of Tennessee Williams, "upon the kindness of strangers." E.T. didn't sing, but if he had he would have raised his voice to say, "Sometimes I feel like a motherless child . . . a long way from home." E.T., had he taken the time to assess his situation, may have lifted his voice to the sky to say, "I'm going to fly away . . . one of these days . . . I'm going to fly away." When the men with the keys captured him, taking him to the laboratory to dissect him, to open him up in order to find what he was made of, he might have hummed, "You got to walk this lonesome valley . . . you got to walk it by yourself." But E.T., like Dorothy, had friends who came to his rescue. Dorothy returned to Kansas more sensitive, more aware of her world. E.T. returned to space having, I'm sure, a mixed view of earth. Black Americans settled here, making a stand for humanity.

It is an honorable position . . . to be a Black American. Our spirituals teach, "I've been 'buked and I've been scorned. . . . I've been talked about sure as I'm born." We maintained an oral tradition and created a written one. Phillis Wheatley, a slave girl, wrote poetry while others sang our songs. We did both because both are necessary. Hammer, while different from, is not in contrast to, Frederick Douglass. Two Live Crew is in a direct line with Big Mama Thornton and all the other blues singers who sang what is called the "race music." (The "good" people would not allow it in their churches or homes.) But we have survived and thrived because of our ability to find the sacred in the secular. "Oh, pray my wings gonna fit me well," says the song, but whether they fit ill or well, we wear what we have with style.

Style has profound meaning to Black Americans. If we can't drive, we will invent walks and the world will envy the dexterity of our feet. If we can't have ham, we will boil chitterlings; if we are given rotten peaches, we will make cobblers; if given scraps, we will make quilts; take away our drums, and we will clap our hands. We prove the human spirit will prevail. We will take what we have to make what we need. We need confidence in our knowledge of who we are.

America is no longer a nation of rural people. We no longer go to visit Grandmother and Grandfather on the farm in the summer. This is no longer a nation where the daily work is done by the body; the daily work is now performed by the mind. The distance between families is no longer a walk or even a short drive. Families, for that matter, are no longer clear. Biology no longer defines whom we love or relate to. We are now able to make emotional choices. There is so much to be done to prepare earth for the next century. Humans, who are so fearful of change, are in such a radical transition. The literature of Black Americans can lead the way. As we were once thrown into a physical unknown where our belief in the wonder of life helped forge a new nation, we can help lead earth into an emotional unknown and seek acceptance for those who are unique. Our literature shows that humans can withstand the unacceptable and yet still find a way to forgive. Our stories, which once were passed sitting on porches after dinner, spitting tobacco juice at fireflies, as Alex Haley's grandmother did, are now passed through the poems, speeches, stories we have written and recorded.

While a bowl of navy beans is one of my favorite meals (with a bit of cole slaw and corn muffins on the side), I still enjoy a smorgasbord. Sometimes a bit of everything creates an appetite while satisfying a hunger. For all the trouble we now understand the voyage of Columbus to have caused, it must have been exciting to live in an age when we finally began to break into a concept of the whole earth. For sure, we have not done a great job, but we have done a better job than if we had stayed home. This century is rolling on to a close. There is both outer space and inner space to be explored. The literature of Black Americans is, in the words of Stevie Wonder, "a ribbon in the sky." We learn about and love the past because it gives us the courage to explore and take care of the future. *Voyager 2* will not come back . . . it has gone too far away. We will not return, we can only visit. But isn't it a comforting thought to realize that the true pioneer of earth is our people? Isn't it the ultimate challenge to accept responsibility not only for ourselves but for our planet? One day, some identifiable life form will come to earth and ask, "Who are these people . . . these Black Americans?" And we will proudly present our book containing our songs, plays, speeches, and poetry. We will proudly say, "We are the people who believe in the possibilities."

DISCOURSES: AN INTRODUCTION

There are certain things that require celebration: Thanksgiving, Christmas, Easter morning, weddings, maybe even the idea behind the Fourth of July. Things that, well, make us happy for a moment or two. We would normally celebrate birthdays, but folk are so crazy to be young that, after a certain age, birthdays become a topic that intelligent friends sound out carefully before even mentioning. We cautiously ask, "Lost a little weight?" hoping the answer will not be a long recital on illness or, even worse, an entire lecture on blood-pressure numbers, the evils of smoking, and the joy of jogging five miles a day. Health is largely overblown. There are other, more private moments that touch us: a new moon at rise, the sun setting red across the sky, some private joy that we finished stripping the furniture, cleaned the shed, wrote a poem.

Writing is both a public and a private pleasure. We write alone, talking to ourselves, trying to explain the universe in a series of metaphors, hoping to be understood.

We mostly put away our thoughts, satisfied that we have written them. Occasionally we take a chance comparable only to skydiving without a parachute: We say to family, friend or lover: "Look what I wrote."

Parents spoil children. Having been and, in fact, being, both a child and a parent, I remember the utter embarrassment of my mother taking my poor efforts and putting them on walls. Even yet she has things I wrote in my preschool days. I have done the same to my son. Little notes he wrote from vacations, stories from second grade, are neatly framed, gracing my walls. I don't think parents do that to hold on to the child; I think we do it to let the child know we are proud of the effort. The only thing more embarrassing than having to look at and be reminded that once we could neither color within the lines nor spell is . . . well . . . nothing. Where would we be if mothers didn't hold on to scraps? How would we know who we are?

GLASSES: FOR TONI MORRISON

Philosophically we are told the glass is either half full or half empty. I suppose the same could be said for a journey. We are either taking the first step toward or the last step from. Anyone tracing our steps will, indeed, find that our first step is her last; though anyone following in our footsteps may find it difficult to know when the journey began. People will, in other words, ask a poet, "How long does it take you to write a poem?" And the only answer that we can honestly give is, "all my life." People do the same to novelists.

I suppose the difference between the novelist and the poet is that the novelist sees an entire world; the poet only a slice of it. Sure, someone is bound to say, but how do you account for *The Iliad* or *The Odyssey* or *The Song of Roland* or any, in fact, of those long, epic poems that give us a hero and a world? Epics, however, today take the form of films or novels. By the same token, had Toni Morrison written during the age of Homer, *Song of Solomon* would have been recited around the campfires after a grueling battle; would have been added to and subtracted from as "The Saga of Milkman Dead" was told to groups of men reclining with an ale at some tavern; would have been used as an example to inspire young Black males struggling in The Gambia with initiation rituals. Milkman, the classic male, tries to determine his relationship with his mother and his father. His mother says: "What harm did I do you?" His father: "Here are the keys. Own something." His community: "Your day is coming." Isn't Ruth simply trying to complete herself, find the half that was lost when her father died, when she called Milkman into that room? Or is Ruth, by having him suckle at her breasts, trying to immunize Milkman against the evils of this world? Did some primal gene Ruth is hardly aware of tell her to take him to his mother's milk and with that milk immunize him from the hurts that men visit upon each other? He could not hate his mother; she and Pilot were the only people who wanted him to live. He did not wish to hate his father. He needed, in the words of T. S. Eliot, to be taught "to care and not to care . . ./because I cannot turn the stair."

Milkman's odyssey carried him to Virginia where he, in order to claim himself fully, had to lose the only person he freely loved, Pilot. And in the losing, Milkman gained the wisdom of Solomon: Only she who is willing to sacrifice is worthy of the prize. Milkman learned that only when you no longer need a safety net of Guitar, of his father, of someone to adore him, of community respect, of historical certainty, can you learn to fly.

Love, Morrison teaches us, is no better than the lover. Cholly loved Pecola. He was, indeed, the only person who would touch her. Yet his touch, like the touch of any free person, is deadly. Cholly impregnates his daughter, then flees, leaving Pecola to her madness. "A whistling woman and a cacklin' hen," the old proverb says, "come to no good end." Cholly is whistling when we meet him, coming up the road. He has no particular destination in mind, no particular thing he is seeking. In other times Cholly would have boarded a ship for the New World, raped the native inhabitants, collected all the riches he could, then squandered them back in Europe. In other times, Cholly would have gone out with his native Masai to kill a lion, or be killed trying to prove his manhood. In future times, Cholly would have set upon a rocket that would either blow him up or carry him to worlds unseen. But Cholly Breedlove is a Negro. And he is not allowed to have dreams. Isn't Morrison answering Langston Hughes when he asks, "What happens to a dream deferred?" It does, indeed, "dry up like a raisin in the sun." Cholly himself festered, then ran.

I like to think that old Cholly, who is dead when the novel opens, in fact, made something of himself. He was ripe to go off on some affirmative action program, maybe to, say, Holy Cross. He continued to have confusions. He wanted to acknowledge his blackness, but it just didn't seem to, well, pay off. In order to justify his lack of control, maybe old Cholly, well, went to Yale Law. Yale had an affirmative action admission program, and Cholly certainly fit the picture of the pitiful Negro who would try very, very hard. Let's say old Cholly graduated and got a job with some senator, say from Missouri, where he hung a Confederate flag in his office to sort of say, "I'm all right, see?" In that office it finally dawns on Cholly that whatever it means to be Black, it is too painful to support. Cholly turns on Black people with a vengeance. He cannot identify with them. They are losers. Didn't he, after all, put his past behind him? Why can't they? Cholly goes back and reclaims his son. At one point, he even sells his sports car (that the company is recalling) to pay the kid's tuition. Cholly likes dirty movies, though. That is his only visible weakness. He likes to watch them and he likes to talk about them. But only to the young Black women in his office. Only to the women he feels have rejected him. Only to the women he knows have less power than he. Cholly goes around giving speeches, laughing at his family. He has found his father and takes pride in not speaking to him. He takes pride in his mother's not having running water in her home. He rejoices and revels in his sister's needing public assistance. He is the darling of the New Right. Sure, he has to hear the nigger jokes and laugh. They, after all, cannot be about him; he's not a nigger. He is a chosen one. He marries Miss Ann. He, in fact, gets a nice dowry since no other man would take her. And he doesn't mind so much when, as they climb into their twin beds and turn out the lights, she says, "Cholly, smile. So I can see where you are." After all, he is her husband and has rights if he chose to assert them. And hey, success costs something. Why don't those other Negroes listen to him and try to understand?

Poor Cholly is rewarded for his faithful service. He is appointed to the Supreme Court. All he has to do is shift his eyes, shuffle his feet, and lie like hell about the one Black woman who dared to say: "This man has no character." Everybody loved the show. Highest ratings since the Nixon scandals. Cholly loved humiliating the Black woman. That will show them about turning him down. She should have said yes. His white folks came through for him! That will show all the Black women to mess with a Black man. Of course, the fact that Black women had done nothing to him would never enter his mind. Which he lost. As he stood to be sworn in on the White House lawn when, instead of the U.S. Marine Band breaking into "The Star-Spangled Banner" or "America the Beautiful" or "God Bless America" or any song that indicated how far Cholly had risen, the band played "Old Black Joe." The president was amazed. "I especially requested that song for Cholly," he said as he watched, with puzzlement, the little Black men in the white coats carry Cholly away. "He always had a such a good, wholesome sense of humor. I just don't understand." Pecola, in case there are some of you that haven't followed her career, went to Europe and became the "Queen of the Blues." She settled in Paris and was the toast of the Continent. Remembering the tragic circumstances of her childhood, she dedicated herself to adopting orphans from around the world. Pecola died on a warm day in August just as a younger singer named Aretha Franklin went number one with a cover of a song by Otis Redding: "Respect."

If Cholly was a free man to whom love was a weapon, Sula is a free woman to whom love will be a trap. The only person Sula loved freely and completely was Nel. They were, in fact, opposite sides of the same coin. Perhaps it is not fair to say Sula loved Nel; perhaps it is more accurate to say Nel completed Sula, who was always searching for her other half. "Pig meat," said a voice in lemon yellow pants. And Sula did not know why she responded. She knew she connected with Shadrack. They were both young people under fire. "Private?" the nurse implored. "Pick up the spoon." A spoon is primordial. We use a spoon at the start of our lives and at the end. "I have measured out my life in coffee spoons." Not coffee cups. Not teaspoons. Coffee spoons. How American. But why were they calling

Shadrack "private?" Private, he thought, was something secret. Was he a secret? Morrison is telling us yes, of course, the Black man is a secret. And his secret is that he must organize death; must order insanity to appear once a year so that it can be controlled. Must be in control of the unstable desires of the people among whom Black Americans find themselves. The privates of the Black man are an open secret. Something to be taken from him and burned, dried up, hung out for everyone to see. Take the privates from a Black man, Morrison says, and white folks feel that they will be safe.

But there is *Sula*. How shall we control her? The novel portrays Sula as the force of evil. It is, the novelist tells us, the community's way of organizing its life. If there is a visible object to hate, then love will be possible. The people of Appalachia have or had a person whom they called the Sin Eater. At death this man would come around and eat the fruit symbolic of the sins of the deceased. Then the deceased could go to heaven. The Sin Eater is an untouchable. Much like the hangman; much like the untouchables of India. Much like any leper. If we are not like "them," then we must be like "us." Sula stands in for every white hurt the community has experienced. She and Shadrack organize the community by being themselves outside it. The good cannot do this. The good, the faithful, the intelligent, the kind, only inspire guilt and anger. It takes a concept of evil to unite a people.

I have, personally, always been amazed that in all of humankind's wars we have never fought over the devil. You can't even get a good conversation started about the devil. Everyone understands you and everyone agrees. But God? You can go off on crusades to slay the infidels; you can be put on racks and flayed to be made to accept a God in which you do not believe; you can be run from one country to the next in order to be free to practice your religion, but it never will occur to you to let others have the same freedom. God is an ideal, but evil is real. We do not always know the guises of God, but we always know the devil. Sula was fine playing the devil's advocate. She had a function. Until she met her true other half. She was an artist without a canvas until the canvas appeared. Then she became confused. She wanted to protect and define him. She wanted to own him because she wanted to have herself completed. Robert Frost teaches us, "Good fences make good neighbors." The same is true of love. Sethe learned to love a little bit so that there would be something left over for the next one. Sula loved as completely as she disdained. Like her grandmother Eva, Sula knew that to name things is to control them. Eva named the Deweys and changed not only their personalities but their physical characteristics: "Theys all Deweys to me." And Sula named Eva "old" and sent her to a nursing home. Eva named Plum dead and burned him up while he was still a man. Sula watched Hannah burn because she was "interested." But Sula could not name nor claim Ajax. He was a free man freely loving a free woman. When Sula was no longer free, Ajax left, leaving Sula with his license so that she could know she did not know his name. I love that. A Black man with a license. Who else to leave it to but the woman he would not license to love him? But Nel never got with the program. Jude didn't want her; he wanted to feel like a man. He wanted Michael Jackson's "Muscles." He wanted the sweat, the bruises, the injuries of a man. He whimpered off to Detroit to hang out in gay bars . . . and refuse to dance. Nel lost them both. Because one needed her; and one needed to use her. Sula and Jude defined themselves by Nel; but Nel's other half was Sula. "We was girls together. Girl, Girl, Girl," Nel cries for all the lost love. And all the time wasted.

Jadine is not a woman to waste time. Jadine wants none of it. Like Phillis Wheatley, Jadine recognizes that in order to live she must unshackle the past. Wheatley had to ask herself: Whom will I hate . . . the seller or the buyer? Wheatley had to ask herself: Since this is my condition, what have I gotten from it? Wheatley wrote a poem to George Washington wishing him well on his quest for freedom. Perhaps she, Wheatley, would never know that freedom, but she was in a place, called the United States, where personal freedom was recognized; where the Enlightenment was more than just a phrase. Where education was possible to order and control the prejudices and superstitions of humankind.

Jadine will not be a good daughter, a good colored girl, a good woman. She will go forth into a great unknown and claim herself. Son is hardly worth it. Certainly he had no appreciation of Jadine's need to claim education for herself. He can fuck like a star, but this is a man fighting the future. Jadine tried to be a good lover to him. Wanted "the brother" to shape up, but he was a Mandinka warrior who could not understand that the wars are over. He loves his first dime, never realizing the diamond he slept next to. Morrison tells me only her mother and I love Jadine. But *Tar Baby* is a perfect novel. Morrison said in an interview some years ago that "the language must not sweat." There is not a wasted word in *Tar Baby*. From the river that lost its way to the couples who live in its wake. The white couple and the Black couple are tied together. They know each other's secrets; but Jadine is an orphan. Like Cholly, like Son, like Sula. Only she will not play out her own destruction. If Son is all the world offers her, she will admit to being alone. And Son will go lickety-split into a place a blind woman takes him.

Morrison does wonderful things with groups of women: the women of Mobile; the women of New York. Such a contrast. The women of Mobile are prototypical women. They do the right things for all the correct reasons against their own better nature. The women of New York strut. Know that they own the city. Know they are making a place safe for themselves. We get the great line from the women of New York: The Black woman is both a ship and a safe harbor. What a wonderful thing to be. Everything. We all know "it's not the size of the ship, but the motion of the ocean" that completes the ultimate intimacy. Morrison says that the Black woman is both. That level of control can either destroy or create. Jadine flies. My students tell me, when we study *Tar Baby,* that Jadine will always be alone. That she will be lonely and by herself. Surely if you are a ship and a safe harbor, you can journey to places unknown. Jadine flies. She does not fool herself that the white folks love her. She does not fool herself that life will somehow become easier. She just remembers that bitch in heat in Baltimore that she tried to save. She could not save the dog, but she can save herself. Jadine flies . . . like a bird in the sky.

Birds, contrary to popular belief, are not free. If you cut down a tree in which a Robin has made her home, the bird will fly a pattern around the area until, exhausted, she falls to the ground. Birds have no ability to adjust because they are territorial creatures. Bound by their home and their space. Environmentalists tell us never to cut a tree in spring. It makes sense. Cut a tree when the birds are not there. Otherwise not only the tree but the surrounding critters and creatures will die. Waiting for its return.

When Adam and Eve left the Garden of Eden, the child they conceived was Sethe. Morrison conceived a Sethe to tell her story of slavery. *Beloved* looks at the "peculiar institution" from the viewpoint of the slave. Some slave sang a song about "Oh freedom over me . . . and before I'll be a slave I'll be buried in my grave and go home to my Lord and be free." "No more auction block for me . . . no more . . . no more." "Flee as a bird . . . to your mountain." Someone had already told the story of Sethe . . . but not in a novel. Morrison offers her biggest challenge to American letters with *Beloved*. If she has taken Sethe's point of view, who will speak for the School Master and his nephews?

It must be very troubling to be a white man. When one considers the fears and superstitions of the European male, it is, in the words of the king of Siam, a "puzzlement." You can see caveman with an erection. Something within him says, "I want a woman." He forces a strong, erect organ in, and out comes something skimpy and damp. You can see the sort of myths that would emerge from that initial experience. She must have done something to me. Why didn't I come out the same way I went in. You could also easily see the confusion when, some nine months later, she produces a child. Surely he had something to do with that. But what? Mankind continues to evolve. They notice that the women bleed at certain times. What could that mean? And if he forces his organ into her at those times, all he gets is blood and this skimpy thing. She must be unclean and unsafe. It could not be he. It could never be he. There must be a perfect man somewhere who did not have to be brought to us this way. There must be a perfect man somewhere whose mother is undefiled. There must surely be a possibility of virgin birth where God simply gives the word and we sinners will be released from the burdens of the flesh. European male, African male, Asian male, all sought freedom from women. All consider woman inferior. All fear the power of the vagina. Freud was wrong. There is no penis envy; there is vaginal envy. The penis, no matter what the myth, is an entity. No matter what its length or width, it is finite. The vagina is a space. It knows no boundary. I have never had difficulty with the story of Adam and Eve because I have never believed it. Any snake in that garden had to be connected to Adam. It was not knowledge but carnal knowledge that Adam forced upon Eve that caused the troubles. The uncoiled snake was somewhere south of Adam's belly button. In a male effort to control, marriage was created. Marriage is not a female institution because it does so little good for women. It labels women outside the institution witches, who are then ripe for burning. Whores who are then ripe for sexual exploitation. It labels the women outside the institution dykes who are then ripe for hating. And with such hateful options facing women, it makes any male better than none. "It cost me a lot but there's one thing that I've got is my man," the song says. "Happiness is just a thing called Joe." You would think the enlightened man would rebel at such images of themselves. But if Susan Brownmiller was right that "all men benefit from rape," it is certainly clear that all men benefit from both the ideal and the institution of marriage. A woman should belong to somebody. She is a prize to be won, spoils to be taken; is a concubine to be visited.

The white man in America must have a special prob-

lem. If the relationship of the male to his penis is alien-
ation, then the white American male faces a particular and
difficult task. What has this organ, which they freely admit
they cannot control, produced? If someone tells you they
have troubled skin that they "just can't do a thing with,"
why, we offer options: drink more water, eat fresh vege-
tables, don't pick your pimples, use Clearasil. If someone
tells you they have trouble with their hair and "can't do a
thing with it," we offer shampoos, oils, brushing rituals.
Hell, if your teeth fall out, we make you new ones. If your
eyes fail, we give you glasses. If you can't use your arms or
legs, we offer therapy. But if you can't control your penis
. . . we blame the women. The white American male under
the sway of this same organ had to reconcile the unrecon-
cilable. When he forces his penis into a white woman, she
produces a white child. When he forces his penis into
a Black woman, she produces a slave. How could one
organ be responsible for two such different entities? One
human to be cared for and nurtured; one a product,
much like wheat or corn or cotton, to be cut down to
size and sold. How does the white American male live with
an organ that is not only not in his control but outside
the control of nature? There has to be a great fury at
himself for his lack of understanding. Why won't his penis
be consistent? The Black man always produces a black
child. The Asian, the American Indian—every other man
produces a human being . . . all the time: Why can't he?
And who will explain it to him? The greatest challenge
of the twenty-first century will be reconciling the human
male to his penis. Morrison has opened the dialogue
with *Beloved:* Sethe will not produce a slave. The white
novelists must now take up that crucible. And shoulder

the responsibilities of all their children.

The writer's life is, I think, a good life. Whether the glass is half full or half empty, we do not cup our hands, letting the essence of life dribble through our fingers. We walk boldly to the fountain and drink deeply.

MISS PIERSALL

Miss Piersall. We were all afraid. Sure, some of the class felt confident, and Miss Piersall was actually a friend of my parents, but somehow fourth grade would be different. For one thing, she kept a long ruler on her desk; for another, it was said she didn't like recess. I wasn't too much worried about the work; the teacher told you what to do and you did it. You couldn't watch television or read your own books until homework was done. My mom taught third grade, but I usually beat her home. My homework was waiting for her, and on my days to do so the dusting and dishes were done; the garbage taken out; Duke, our dog, was fed. It's not that I was a "good" girl so much as I couldn't, and can't, stand being fussed at. And worse than the words was that "you've-let-me-down" look. I hated that look more than anything.

One day Miss Piersall had teacher's meeting. I attended St. Simon's Episcopal School, and the nuns liked to meet during the day. The instructions to the students were: no talking. I didn't talk, but the fourth grade could be heard all over the building. When Miss Piersall came back to class she was very angry. "I'm going to give each one of you a swat," she said. I raised my hand. "Nikki?" "I wasn't talking, Miss Piersall. I shouldn't be swatted," I said. "But you know who was, don't you?" Which didn't seem fair to me. Of course I knew. But I didn't tell. And I was given one swat.

I am a writer because I believe fairness should be accorded the individual.

MEATLOAF:
A VIEW OF POETRY

Poetry, to me, is the association of disassociated ideas. I like clear simple images, clear simple metaphors, making clear simple statements about not-so-clear, not-so-simple human beings. In other words, I believe poets like Robert Frost are apt to be highly underrated. I want my students to tell me a story poetically. I am not especially interested in their love lives, because young people, in my mind, don't have love lives, they have lust lives and stressful social lives, but they are far too young to know, let alone knowledgeably talk about, love. I have seldom read an interesting poem about the discovery of raindrops, or clouds floating by, or sunsets either, so we eliminate these categories. I start my classes by asking the favorite poem of each student in my class. Surprisingly enough, there are a number of students who do not have favorite poems; who cannot even lie about it. I ask for favorite poets and run into the same problem. I then, quite naturally, ask the class why it is taking my course. The answers are heartening and dismaying.

Why, which is a real question, do we think we can teach people to write poetry? Why would we want to do that if we could? I don't think we can, and I don't think we should. It's not as if there isn't an abundance of poets running about—in fact, the market is saturated with them—but poetry is an art, not an academic exercise. Poetry is the way we look at life and the conclusions we draw. Mostly, if I teach anything, I teach my students to think and to talk about their thoughts. How, you may legitimately ask, do I teach them to think? I don't think thinking is an exercise. It is something that if we do it two mornings a week for one hour and fifteen minutes, the habit might stick. Most young people want poetry to be math or science or history. A subject. If they put the right metaphors in the right place with the right number of syllables to a line, they will have a poem. I don't think so. I believe if they put enough passion into a real subject, they may stumble onto a poem.

All poetry is written in the vernacular. The olden poets wrote of and in their times. We must do the same. Will that mean that some of our images are "That sucks"? I think so. Some will use "shitty," some will say "motherfucker," because that's a part of our vernacular. Will it offend? You bet. But poets who don't offend are not doing their job. There is no right or wrong in my classroom; only what works or doesn't work for the poet and the poem. That, I admit, frustrates my class, because the students are used to being told what to do and how to do it. I think it's unmitigated crap that anyone in school—elementary, junior, high, or college—can produce a writer. We can produce junior assholes who think they can write and are therefore exempt from the rule of general civilization; we can produce youngsters and teachers who form cliques thinking they are the best and the brightest and don't have to engage in the daily cares of the world in which they live; but I hope I don't do that.

I hope, by discussing sports and homelessness, race and current television, world news, scientific wonders, and anything else that comes to mind, that I am showing my students they must contemplate the world in which they live. I believe their responsibility as writers is to have as much sympathy for the rich as for the poor; as much pity for the beautiful as for the ugly; as much interest in the mundane as in the exotic. Meatloaf is a wonderful thing as worthy of a poem as any spring day or heroic deed. The exercise I try to instill is: Look; allow yourself to look beyond what *is*, into what *can be*, and more, into what *should be*. Poems are dreams. Dream. But dreams are conceived in reality. Meatloaf is real. Write that poem.

EARTHLINGS: THE FUTURE TRADITION

Growing up in the Western tradition, which isn't really so much "Western" as an amalgam of all cultures, one can't help but admire Jesus. As a Christian reared in the Baptist and Episcopalian faiths, I always did, and still do, love the story of the boy in the temple assailing the elders. One of my favorite songs is "Peace Be Still," which tells the journey of the ship on the storm-tossed Sea of Galilee. I'm especially fond of the story of Nicodemus sneaking around at night to let Jesus know he did, indeed, believe but . . . well . . . maybe it was too much trouble to say so in the light. Of course, Jesus was killed. He rose on Easter and we are all happy. But He did die and that was sad. I used to cry each Easter season when we did the Stations of the Cross. It just galled me that Peter denied Him. That the crowd screamed, *"Give us Barabbas!" That* Pilate was such a gutless wonder that he, like Lady MacBeth, thought he could wash his hands of it all. In *King of Kings,* the talkie version, there was always one voice in the crowd asking,

"What has this man done?" I identified with that. I liked to think that had I been in the crowd, I would at least have cried out, "What has He done?"

Socrates was a great favorite of mine because he wanted to teach the young people. I know now that he wanted to teach the boys, but when I was told about him by my grandfather I always thought there were girls as well as boys there. I always saw a group of kids sitting under an olive tree, answering questions this wise man would ask. Of course, we killed him. The town didn't want the young people to know anything. I could understand that. Adults frequently changed the conversation when I came into the room, but no one, as far as I could see, was ever made to take poison because she slipped and mentioned a divorce or a pregnancy or someone "running around" with someone else's husband. Frankly, I didn't see why Socrates didn't just "had up," as we say in the Black community, hit the road. Find a better place. But I was a child. And children think you can move on; adults know better. So Socrates died a noble death and his star pupil moved on and we were told we were the better. I think not. The crowd, once again, was wrong.

It's impossible for me not to love Galileo. He was the first modern, true rebel. The Church said he was wrong, and he went: *"Fuck it; I'm wrong."* He recanted. He refused to die because people were too stupid to understand what he was talking about. He knew he was right. But so did Jesus; so did Socrates. Though only Galileo refused to die. It took about five hundred years before anyone admitted Galileo had been wronged, but a late admission is, I suppose, better than none. Guerilla warfare began at that point. Whatever else Galileo gave us, he said clearly: It is better to live on than to die in fruitless battle.

180

I'm not trying to fight any sort of religious war here, nor do I fail to admire the deeds and aspirations of divine beings. It is simply that the lesson I learned from these three men was that the people are frequently wrong because they tend to follow stupid leaders who indulge the people in outdated and outlandish folklore and superstition.

I am a Black American poet. I am female. I am, at this writing, forty-eight years old. I am a daughter, a mother, a professor of English. I like grilled rack of lamb and boiled corn on the cob . . . Silver Queen when I can get it. I like television and sports. I love bid whist. I smoke cigarettes and, should the occasion arise, will have a glass of red wine, preferably Merlot. I like my mother, my sister, my son, and my dogs. I will drink any hot, black liquid that someone will call coffee. I hate diet soda, seat belts, anti-smokers, pro-lifers, and stupid people who think they have any right to tell me how to live. I have no need to control anyone and will not be controlled. I believe that if I keep examining my life and what I think and feel, I will have added one, teeny, tiny bit of truth to this planet I call home. It is inconceivable that I feel alienated from Western tradition; my people have contributed so much that is vital and good to it. I am alienated from the *people* who call themselves white, who think they own Western tradition.

Why I write poetry is still largely an unknown. It's something that I think I can do. What I absolutely know is that it had to be my decision. I remember writers coming to Fisk University when I was an undergraduate. Other students would, invariably, give copies of their work to the writers. What they were actually hoping for, I don't honestly know. To me, people who do things like that really believe Lana Turner was discovered sitting on a stool in a drugstore. They must really think there is something called an overnight success. That one day you were happily walking down the street, maybe going to the grocery store for some milk or a pack of cigarettes, when . . . boom! Some guy steps out and says, "You should be in pictures." Off you run to Hollywood and live happily ever after. Or you give a poem to Gwen Brooks or Langston Hughes. They return to Chicago or Harlem. Tired from the journey, they venture into the kitchen and open the refrigerator. Ah, they are in luck. There is cold fried chicken from Sunday's meal. And . . . gracious . . . a slice of apple pie. They put the coffeepot on and sit at the kitchen table. But . . . they have nothing to read. But wait . . . didn't that kid in Nashville give them a collection of poems, or was it short stories? They, on tired feet, most likely swollen ankles, walk back to their briefcases. Yes. There it is. "My Poems" by a kid. Why, hot damn, this is great stuff. Forget about eating. They curl up in their favorite armchair and read on. Dawn is peeking through the shades. How could the time have passed? They call their agent who comes right over to read for himself. Yes, this kid must be published . . . right away. The kid goes on to win the Yale Younger Writers Series . . . is asked to join the Society of Poets and represents the United States in the USA/USSR Poetry International Conference. And to think he almost didn't show his work because he was shy. Ahhhh . . . happy endings.

Except, I think not. I think artists have to take responsibility for their work. There is no magic out here. Only a lot of hard work and very little reward. The great writers whom we venerate today were hardly known in their time; or were, like Shakespeare, wildly popular and therefore scorned by the scholars. Am I alienated from Western tradition? Hardly. It taught me that no matter what you are doing, some folk will like it and some will hate it. But mostly it taught me that the critics and scholars are wrong. Which means one must always be wary of praise and always put criticism in perspective. Since I have little personal regard for what are called "leaders," whether of the race or the muse, one must get to the people who might appreciate and understand what one is saying and beyond the leaders who would control and trap you for their own limited ends.

Preachers, of course, only preach to the saved. Each Sunday in every church they may rail and rally against the sinners, but they are preaching to the saved. Folk sit in church and k-n-o-w, "We are not like *them*," whoever them are. Up to and including, I should imagine, Baptists, Methodists, Catholics, Episcopalians, Presbyterians, snake handlers, holy rollers, and any other segment of their own religion, let alone Buddhism, Islam, Judaism, voodoo, animism, and other beliefs far different. Opera singers only sing to those who come to the opera. Certainly there are operas on radio and, occasionally, television, but let a good ol' boy hit *Aida* by mistake and watch that dial turn like a rabbit seeing a dog in the field. Quick. Poets are like that, too. We are listened to and read only by people who like poetry. Men have been known to turn down lewd and obscene physical acts on their bodies rather than come to poetry readings. And we all know men will do almost anything for a lewd and obscene act. I have wondered why poets get into these petty quarrels when there are so very few of us and even fewer folk who care what we think.

If it weren't so pitiful, it would be funny to hear human males discoursing on why women don't write poetry. Some of us believe that the creation of language itself

183

belongs to women. While the men were on all fours grunting around in the fields, we women were drawing pictures on the caves, putting decorations on the clay bowls in the savannah, walking around holding our children, developing the hoe and the rake, collecting seeds and learning the planting seasons. I mean, it is so illogical to think that any system that intended to support life first created "man." However would it perpetuate itself? Female has to come first. I'm sure the first man who tried to appropriate civilization was laughed out of the village. I know the first times the Africans saw white people they thought the whites were dead . . . were ghosts . . . and the Africans thought them uncivilized. Just as we have now come to the point that some of the conservative men—George Will and Walter Williams come to mind immediately—despite all their male chauvinism, have to fight for the rights of their daughters, we can easily see how the human female fought, thousands of years ago, for the right of her son to read, draw, plant, and be privileged to the knowledge of medicine. Had she only anticipated T. S. Eliot and his arrogant exclusiveness, she might have had second thoughts. But I don't blame T. S. He had enough self-blame in his life to do without mine. We have this guy here, Eliot, from St. Louis. Already you can see the problem. The most vital parts of St. Louis are on the riverfront, which is populated by Black people. His mother wanted him to be a gentleman? Why? And if he was to please her he had to turn his back on everything that was exciting. He had to make himself into what he thought was a "Western" man . . . and, having worked so hard at it, found the United States wanting and moved to England. This is a guy whose best friend and mentor is certifiably insane. Without Pound, where would Eliot be? And how does Pound fit into "tradition"? That same Pound was a fascist, or he didn't mind saying he was a fascist. I'm not against Ezra. Like an old woman selecting yams, Pound picked talent. And he found the strong, durable ones who would feed the family tonight and still seed for next spring. But is this Western tradition? White men mentoring white men to the exclusion of all others certainly is.

Deutschland über alles. But is this good? Is it right? I agree with the women who say no. Common sense would tell anyone, white men included, that when the natives begin to question the system . . . the system is dead. Melvin Tolson, that wonderful Black poet, wrote three lines that I will always remember: "When the skins are dried/the flies will go home." And, "We judge a civilization only in its decline." I was a junior in college when I was privileged to hear Tolson read; he died the next year, and those three lines jumped at me. Of course, I said to myself, of course. At the same conference Lerone Bennett, Jr., pointed out: "The last bastion of white supremacy is in the Black man's mind." I don't know if Lerone meant man and woman, but he said man. I know and I knew what my generation had uncovered. Rap Brown said it best: "The whole honkie situation is through." I like that. Not white civilization, not Western civilization, not even Eurocentric civilization, but the honkie situation.

To agree that the end is upon us is not, however, to deny the journey. Human civilization is composed of human cultures. Some of those cultures are worthy of emulation, as long as it is understood that we emulate the values, not the rewards, of that culture. The West has given the world the idea of the individual. For a variety of reasons far too numerous to attempt to explain in this essay, America turned away from tribalism to the rights and responsibilities of the individual. It has taken this Western outpost these many years to include white women, let alone people of color, under the banner of "these truths we hold self-evident." Simply because the practice falls short of the ideal is no particular reason to reject the dream. No, I am not alienated from Western tradition, because I am, and my people have been, too much a part of it. The writers may write, the politicians may legislate, the preachers may hope, and the scientists may try to prove otherwise . . . but whatever is Western, not to mention tradition, belongs to me. We can be read out of the will, but the deceased is still dead. As that oldest of Western traditions informs us: "The king is dead. Long live the king." Just as nature abhors a vacuum, humans resist change. Change will occur; vacuums will be filled. And Western tradition, which started in the East and moved west, will in westward movement end up in the East and move once again west. We are all a part of the earth . . . earthlings . . . and we will one day push so far out that we will reach the ends of this universe, this galaxy, this wonderful star and, instead of the arrogance, domination, and guns of insecure people, say, "Hello. I am an earthling. I am from the third planet of the yellow sun. It is traditional with us to extend a hand of friendship and welcome."

APPALACHIAN ELDERS:
THE WARM HEARTH WRITER'S
WORKSHOP

The year was 1964. It was a fine spring afternoon. Big white puffs of cumulus clouds floated in a clear sky of blue. It was a day to sit on a hill and chew on a blade of grass, giving vent to the muse if you were a poet; it was a day to haul old clothes, mismatched dishes, half-empty, dried-up paint in cans . . . junk . . . out of the garage and maybe clean some gutters if you were a husband; a day for frying whitefish with potatoes and onions and a few hush puppies on the side to go with the apple pies you had already baked if you were a mother. It was a day to drive your sister's brand new Fiat 1100 D. I was just a student then, not a poet. I drove the car.

I only wanted to go to Kroger's. Gary was home visiting for my twenty-first birthday. I didn't need to go far nor for much, but since I was going, Mommy gave me a list. Gary's son, Christopher, was too little to help, but since I was going could he ride? I insisted Mommy come with me, since it was her list and she hadn't ridden in the car. Gary stayed home.

Everything went as it should. I hadn't driven a five-speed in years, but I got safely out of first and on the road. We lived in Lincoln Heights, which does not have a chain grocery store, requiring us to travel to Lockland, our neighboring community to the south. I drove out the long way, taking Springfield Pike through Wyoming, cutting back to Lockland via Wyoming Avenue.* The car was wonderful. The 1100 D was like a little box. Hers was powder blue. We shopped and loaded the three bags onto the backseat. Chris was in the corner.

The direct way home is Wayne Avenue. I never did like to travel Wayne Avenue because there's nothing to look at. No significant trees, no opening vistas. But it was the direct route and the logical thing to do. Between Kroger's and home there is a stoplight at Wyoming and Wayne, a stoplight just in front of the funeral home, one 4-way stop sign at the gas station and new factory, a stoplight at Medosch, and a stoplight at the top of the hill. I cruised along at a decent speed, as the Fiat was not a fast car. Traffic flowed smoothly for a Saturday. It was way too early for the cruisers and drunks who turned Wayne Avenue into a strip after dark. I had just reached the top of the hill when the light turned amber. Normally I would have simply gone on around the corner, but my mother and nephew were with me and I didn't necessarily want Mommy to think I drove with abandon. I came to a full stop. Then I heard the most awful sound in the universe. A car that had not even been close enough behind me for me to have noticed it started hitting its brakes. I could tell he was not going to make it. I saw, clearly, his rubber on the pavement. I saw his crazed eyes trying to stop his car. I saw us being hit . . . and then we were.

* Wyoming, Lockland, and Woodlawn are suburbs of Cincinnati.

He came dead-on at us, knocking the Fiat sideways into the two lanes of traffic. I could feel the car scrunch under the blow. The back just seemed to fold under. I remember turning the engine off and riding the impact out. It all took seconds. My first real thought was Chris. He was shocked and scared but all right. I turned to Mommy, who was shaken but unhurt. The left side of the car had caved in also, and my leg was trapped. The car was totaled.

All the normal things were done. Police were called. The driver who hit us was a drunk and from out of town. No insurance. We, however, were covered. My ankle was hurt and swollen, but I guess we were all so happy no real damage was done that we went home, filed the necessary papers, apologized profusely to Gary, and that should have been that. But it wasn't. I was never to wear a high-heeled shoe again. My toe had been broken.

August 1988 had started with a decision for me. I would have a foot operation. I can't say that I had truly forgotten about the accident, but it was not at the top of my mind. Through the ensuing twenty-seven years I had had foot problems. Many times I simply had to take shoes off because the pain of having anything on my left foot was unbearable. I well remember changing planes in Chicago one winter and taking one shoe off, going from terminal to terminal feeling like "diddle-diddle dumpling . . . my son John." I had come to southwestern Virginia to accept a position as Visiting Commonwealth Professor in the English Department. I had been invited to stay another year. The dress at Virginia Tech is casual, which probably is an understatement. I had taken to wearing moccasins, whether in business suit or evening dress. It's time to deal with this, I said to myself. And off I went to a foot doctor. Surgery was recommended, but it was summer and I was busy. Since I would be teaching in the fall, why not August? Both my left little toe and my right little toe needed surgery. The good thing was I would finally be pain-free. The bad thing was more pain than I had known since I birthed my son . . . and no crutches.

I, quite honestly, had looked forward to crutches. I had even purchased a long, white, linen skirt that I thought would just flow as I bravely, determinedly made my way about. No. No crutches for me, just two weird-looking wooden shoes.

My foot surgery was done outpatient. You just kind of lie there while he chats with you and grinds your bones. I seriously tried not to think about it. If you've never had someone grind on your bones, I have no metaphor for the pain. The painkillers are only to make your surgeon feel better. They don't do a thing for you. I didn't whimper nor cry nor push him away and leave. I'm so glad we did both feet at once, because I would never have had the second foot done. A friend took me home, propped me up in bed, and made tomato soup for me. She also got my painkillers. I was to be in bed, off my feet, for at least a week. Most likely I looked pitiful. Mommy and Gary sent me flowers with a card that said, "Happy Trails to You." The department sent me flowers saying they missed me. Other friends sent flowers, too. I like to think I brooded among my flowers. That I achieved a sort of poetic angst while I lay in bed contemplating my bound feet. I think, however, that I whimpered. I think I was miserable.

My best friend in the English Department is Ginney Fowler. Ginney was associate head of the department at that time. She took a call from Warm Hearth Retirement Community asking if anyone in English would like to do a writer's workshop with retirees. I don't know if Ginney thought of me because I like old people or because I was laid up in bed and would have agreed to anything that gave me a reason to look forward to being on my feet again. The phone rang, at any rate, and I answered it.

Ginney had to drive me out to Warm Hearth. It is a beautiful collection of buildings set in a glen. The trees whisper to you. Rabbits scamper across the road while the possum ambles and the groundhogs just look up waiting for you to pass. There are birds all around, and some have seen deer. I went up to the third floor. I had not led a workshop of this proposed nature before. As I hobbled in, I noticed the canes and walkers of the people gathered. I was home.

The first thing I wanted to establish was that they did not have to accept me. I told them who I was, read some of my poetry, gave copies of my book to the Warm Hearth library, and asked them to think it over. I am Black and they are not. We agreed to meet the next week.

My thoughts, quite naturally, turned to my grandmother. She was born in Albany, Georgia, but had lived her adult life in Knoxville, Tennessee. She had belonged to the book club, the garden club, the bridge club, and a host of self-help organizations for Negroes. She was a lifelong Democrat, though my grandfather was a Lincoln Republican. I tried to imagine what I'd do if I were conducting a workshop with grandmother, what would I do? The answer was simple. I would do nothing. I would listen and encourage. She would be perfectly capable of telling her own stories.

Our very first reader was Zeke Moore. His story was short and funny. The workshop rather shyly commented on it and, in what turned out to be a wonderful thing, started to say, "Why that reminds me . . ." We had agreed to meet for one hour each Wednesday morning from ten to eleven o'clock. To me, all time is a suggestion. The watch I wear turned around on my left wrist is a gift from my mother who, one cold, winter afternoon when I was supposed to take her to lunch to meet her friend Liz Armstrong, walked out to the carport and sat in the car while I finished my phone conversation. "You know we have to be on time," she said. "Liz has to go back to work." That was Mother's idea of a reprimand. Of course, I felt foolish realizing she was sitting in a cold car waiting for me to drive her, but why did she go out when I was on the phone? Mother, unlike her mother and my father, is not a nagger or a shouter. That Christmas she gave me a watch. It has no numbers on it.

I was late—a lot. But I stayed later. Lunch at Warm Hearth has two seatings. My group ate at noon, giving us a built-in extra time. We could gossip and chat and still get downstairs on time. The one question that kept popping up was, What did I expect of them? There were about twelve of us: two men and ten women. There has seldom been more than two men at one time. I don't understand why.

Some of us have been teachers, some nurses, a preacher, an explorer for oil, farmers, lots of landowners, many housewives, and almost all were parents. Most of us cooked and all of us ate, so I had expected food to play a very prominent role in our writing. Janie Kay wrote a narrative saying she never wanted to cook again; Francis Brown found her grandmother's recipe book. We wrote about our marriages, our lineages, old homes we once lived in, and great homes we visited. Anna Kenney was our only short fiction writer; many of us tried poetry. Mostly we wrote about ourselves.

Gloria Naylor was our first real writer-visitor. She was peppered with questions about agents, selling to television, how she got started. Alex Haley stopped by for a minute and stayed a couple of hours. And brought the press with him.

The workshop had no true idea of me, though I think they liked me. They did, however, have family around the States who would send them some clipping every now and then about me. "Why, you're actually famous," Zeke concluded after he had received a press clipping from Florida. If I have done anything right with the workshop, it is that I started us on equal ground, which is how true relationships should start.

Just about the time my feet had healed, I had to have a hemorrhoid operation. "I am carrying this identification with the workshop too far," I declared. They all had helpful hints and lots of sympathy. (For future workshop leaders only: I am not recommending physical infirmities in order to help your workshop identify with and understand you. It just worked out that way. I also wear bifocals and have dentures. We had bonded.)

One day I was having a bad day, threw on my jeans and a sweatshirt, and went to workshop. "Are you going to a football game?" I was asked. I have dressed properly ever since.

At the end of our first year we had accumulated quite a bit of work. I thought we should do some desktop publishing. Tammy Shepherd, who works with me in the English Department, had been typing our handwritten manuscripts onto a disc. We could have them run off for a minimum amount of money. We purchased folders and bingo! "The Warm Hearth Sampler" was born. The next semester we did the same thing. Then came the inevitable question: When could we publish a "real book"? *Appalachian Elders* is the name of our real book.

What have I learned in these three years we have been together?

To have an effective workshop, you must be patient and supportive.

The workshop should be noncritical. It's all too easy to fall into the habit of noticing how something is said and miss the wonder and beauty of what is said.

Everyone should be encouraged to write, and no one should be pressured.

As workshop leader I do not read my work; I am there for the group. I also read every story that is written and make comments on the copy I return. Some people are shy; it takes them a little longer to trust the group. I think those who need more time should be allowed to take it.

Some of the group does not write. All our members are valuable; both those who write and those who listen. We have also been fortunate in our volunteers. Some of our members cannot write because of arthritis, failing eyesight, and other things of that nature. Having someone to talk the stories to can make a big difference. Cathee Dennison and Connie Wones got us through a very busy first February. Kathy Dickenson started as a volunteer and has become a member.

I have wanted the Warm Hearth story told because all too often the workaday world thinks that world is both the only one and the real one. Too many people think older people have nothing to give. People have thought we were doing oral history. They had no concept that older people who had never written before could take up a new task. Some of our members type; two recently have learned computer; most write by hand. Becky Cox is our typist now, helping us keep track of our work. We have not created any miracles on Wednesdays. We have only come together to share. I am not truly a leader; I am a catalyst. We have had public readings, our annual lunch, one fun dinner party. My mother and aunt have visited us. One member has a daughter who has joined. We have one member who is not living at Warm Hearth. We have lost Charlie, who had been married to Laura for sixty-three years; Zeke, who had a sudden heart attack; and Mancy Adams, who was one hundred and one years old. Janie Kay moved and Francis lost James. But we still have a story to tell. The years and the wonder of life inform our sensibilities. We mostly write about ourselves.

and responsibilities of the individual. It has taken this
Western outpost these many years to include white
women, let alone people of color, under the banner of
"these truths we hold self-evident." Simply because the
practice falls short of the ideal is no particular reason to
reject the dream. No, I am not alienated from Western
tradition, because I am, and my people have been, too
much a part of it. The writers may write, the politicians
may legislate, the preachers may hope, and the scientists
may try to prove otherwise . . . but whatever is Western,
not to mention tradition, belongs to me. We can be read
out of the will, but the deceased is still dead. As that oldest
of Western traditions informs us: "The king is dead. Long
live the king." Just as nature abhors a vacuum, humans
resist change. Change will occur; vacuums will be filled.
And Western tradition, which started in the East and
moved west, will in westward movement end up in the
East and move once again west. We are all a part of the
earth . . . earthlings . . . and we will one day push so far out
that we will reach the ends of this universe, this galaxy, this
wonderful star and, instead of the arrogance, domination,
and guns of insecure people, say, "Hello. I am an earth-
ling. I am from the third planet of the yellow sun. It is
traditional with us to extend a hand of friendship and
welcome."

does Pound fit into "tradition"? That same Pound was a fascist, or he didn't mind saying he was a fascist. I'm not against Ezra. Like an old woman selecting yams, Pound picked talent. And he found the strong, durable ones who would feed the family tonight and still seed for next spring. But is this Western tradition? White men mentoring white men to the exclusion of all others certainly is. *Deutschland über alles*. But is this good? Is it right? I agree with the women who say no. Common sense would tell anyone, white men included, that when the natives began to question the system . . . the system is dead. Melvin Tolson, that wonderful Black poet, wrote three lines that I will always remember: "When the skins are dried/the flies will go home." And, "We judge a civilization only in its decline." I was a junior in college when I was privileged to hear Tolson read; he died the next year, and those three lines jumped at me. Of course, I said to myself, of course. At the same conference Lerone Bennett, Jr., pointed out: "The last bastion of white supremacy is in the Black man's mind." I don't know if Lerone meant man and woman, but he said man. I know and I knew what my generation had uncovered. Rap Brown said it best: "The whole honkie situation is through." I like that. Not white civilization, not Western civilization, not even Eurocentric civilization, but the honkie situation.

To agree that the end is upon us is not, however, to deny the journey. Human civilization is composed of human cultures. Some of those cultures are worthy of emulation, as long as it is understood that we emulate the values, not the rewards, of that culture. The West has given the world the idea of the individual. For a variety of reasons far too numerous to attempt to explain in this essay, America turned away from tribalism to the rights

VI

POSTSCRIPT:

"FALALALALALALALALA"

—TRADITIONAL

Christmas will just have to hold its horses. I'm not ready. Oh yes, I know everybody is so used to my efficiency that this is shocking news. After all, I'm the one who has usually finished my shopping by late July and am ready to wrap shortly after Labor Day. Have I learned my lesson, you may ask, remembering the year I had purchased and wrapped but forgot to properly label the gifts? No. It was only minor that my father was given a lovely nightgown I had purchased in Rome and my son received a wonderful box of Cuban cigars I had legally purchased in East Berlin, though sort of illegally brought into the United States. Mommy would not have noticed the difference, since she likes checkers, if the whole computer had not come with the game. These things, after all, do happen. No. Christmas will have to wait, not because I'm not capable of being ready . . . I have chosen not to be ready.

Let's face it. I was awake last December 26 at 5:30 A.M. anyway. We have five dogs (one for each lap, as my nephew says), and someone has to feed them. I know some folks think dogs lead cushy lives lying around the house all day, only really working when the mailman or meter reader comes around, but I don't agree. Dogs have a hard life. How would you feel if you, once a proud canine of the wild who chased his own rabbit for dinner, who reared his children in the collective ways of the group, now found yourself with three old ladies and two boys, or rather young men, whose idea of exercise is turning over a log or two on the fireplace? How would you feel having your world be restricted by a high fence with ivy winding its way down, and the cats, who once ran at the very thought of you, balleting along the trellis, laughing at your attempts to get your teeth into them? Now don't get me wrong, I'm not against cats, though it does seem not quite right that dogs have to be leashed and cats run free. But the real question is, How would you feel if you had no discernible reason to be? No real job to do; no place that was expecting you to show up at a certain time and perform a real function? You know how you would feel. Terrible. We know enough about people not having real jobs and how that deteriorates the personality to know that our poor dogs must feel, on most days, positively useless. Yet, they forge through, keeping themselves clean and occupied days upon end, watching *Jeopardy!* and *Wheel* and an occasional murder mystery with us. Are they truly interested in these things? I doubt it, but that's their day, and they accept it with a grace we all could learn from. I am still old-fashioned and southern enough to think living things should start their day with a hot meal, so I am always up by five-thirty to microwave their dog food with whatever scraps I can find in the fridge. My sister, by the way, worries that they will get fat and die before their time; I worry that they will be hungry and kill us before ours.

So I am up in time to make the Macy's after-Christmas sale, is my point. I could, last year, actually have been first or second in line at the door. The previous year I was in the first ten and made some wonderful purchases on wrapping paper, ornaments, Christmas cards, and an electronic pencil sharpener, which also opens letters. I have chosen not to go that route again. Am I getting lazy, you may wonder? My son came home from the army to discover I had purchased a red, two-seater sports car in his absence. He was both delighted and perturbed. Delighted because, after all, there is a sports car in the family; perturbed because I was not letting, nor interested in letting, him drive it. He agreed one morning to go to the grocery store with me because "those bags can be mighty heavy," and as we were trying to get from our side street into the main road I prudently waited until traffic abated. "Gosh, Mom," says the now-mature but still-adventuresome I've-been-in-the-army-two-years son, "you've really lost your edge." Lost my edge? Because I won't go running out into the insane, nay, suicidal, driving of Virginia? "Well, I better drive back or we'll never get home." I felt my car give a shudder. I know cars aren't supposed to cry, but they do. Especially when they are purchased by little old lady poets and now know they will be given a real workout by a young man with no regard for payments, insurance, scratches . . . all the things that inhibit mothers from burning rubber. No. I have not lost my edge nor am I lazy. I just have begun to think that things should be savored, slowed down, really slowly gone through, in order to be enjoyed.

I have traveled for a living most of my life. It's only been in the last few years, after my son graduated from high school, that I could actually afford a regular job with medical benefits, life insurances, and whatnot. I have learned, working a regular job with regular hours in a regular office and classroom, why you need medical benefits, however. My blood pressure, which has been low my entire life, is now up. Seeing the same people every day is really a lot of pressure, but that's another discussion. When you travel a lot you have to get ahead of things, or most assuredly you will be behind. I had to get the birthday cards out early or I would forget; I had to have Valentine's Day candy ordered for my mother or I would find myself in the only town in America that does not have express wire service. I had to have my turkey for Thanksgiving delivered and in the freezer, and quite naturally I had to have everything ready for Christmas or I would find myself on Christmas morning explaining that I meant to get to the store to pick up the wonderful gift that could not be lived without. No more.

Last year we overdosed. Everybody got everybody everything that was ever mentioned. Obscene is not too strong a word. If one more gift had come into the house, we would have needed to reinforce the floor. Did we think the world was coming to an end? Did we foresee some tragedy? I don't know, but December 26, over coffee and the lightest dollar pancakes a sister ever made, we had a discussion. Next year we would make choices. We will only give one gift to each person. We will have a limit on how much we can spend. Each person can only cook one dish. Is this going to be rough? You bet, because now we all have to think; now we will have to make choices. Yet, that is, to me and, really, to the family, the essence of Christmas. Jesus was born to give us a choice; we humans could continue to be controlled by fate or we could accept the Savior and be redeemed. We humans may not always control the circumstances of our bodies, but we can control our souls. That's what is so nice about Christmas. I think

I took it too lightly and treated the holiday as a job. Something I needed to get done by a certain time. This year my family and I are getting back to basics. We will be back to telling family stories; back to a half-empty tree with ornaments we have made over the years. The angel on top is the one I made of straws and spray-painted in the first or second grade. We're lucky because Mommy has kept these things. We're stringing popcorn and sharing it with the dogs. This Christmas will be our best ever because we are determined to turn back to the days when it was just us, happy to be together, grateful for the love we share. I shouldn't say I'm not ready for Christmas because I really am. I'm just not ready for the mall to start Christmas sales before the World Series has been played; I'm not ready for my favorite radio station to start the carols; I'm not ready to be told how many more shopping days are left; and I'm definitely not ready for the arguments about putting a manger scene in some city square. I am ready to slow down and be grateful for all the blessings that have been sent our way. I still like Santa Claus and will faithfully leave him some chocolate chip cookies. Only this year, I am taking the time to make them.